LIVING BY

THE SPIRIT

BISHOP ANTONIO M. PALMER

LIVING BY THE SPIRIT

Published by Kingdom Publishing LLC
Odenton, MD 21113

Printed in the U.S.A.

ISBN: 978-1-967006-00-7

Table of Contents

INTRODUCTION

Faith in the Hebrew Messiah, *Yeshua* (Jesus), is a journey that begins with a heart conviction, repentance from sin, and an acceptance that He is Lord and Savior and continues as the believer grows in an intimate, abiding relationship with Him. This transformative process is not based on human effort alone but is made possible by the indwelling and active work of the Holy Spirit. The apostle Paul declares, *"If we live in the Spirit, let us also walk in the Spirit"* (Galatians 5:25, NKJV), emphasizing that spiritual life is both initiated and sustained by the Spirit of God. Yet, many believers struggle to understand how to live by the Spirit and experience the fullness of God's presence in their daily lives.

This book, *Living By The Spirit*, seeks to guide believers through the essential aspects of developing a Spirit-led life. From the moment of regeneration—when the Holy Spirit imparts new life—to the ongoing process of sanctification, every step of the believer's journey is shaped by His presence and power (John 3:5-6; Titus 3:5). The Holy Spirit convicts, teaches, comforts, empowers, and leads believers into spiritual maturity, enabling them to walk in righteousness and fulfill their divine calling (Romans 8:14; John 16:13).

Developing an intimate relationship with God requires more than intellectual understanding; it necessitates a deep, abiding fellowship with the Holy Spirit. Jesus Himself assured His disciples that the Spirit would dwell within them, teaching and reminding them of all truth (John 14:16-17, 26). This abiding relationship is cultivated through prayer, worship, obedience, and a sensitivity to the Spirit's leading. As believers yield to the Spirit, they begin to exhibit the fruit of the Spirit—love, joy, peace, patience, kindness, goodness, faithfulness, gentleness, and self-control (Galatians 5:22-23).

This book is designed to help believers move beyond mere religious activity into a dynamic, Spirit-filled life. Each chapter explores key biblical principles and practical applications to deepen one's walk with God. The goal is to equip believers to move from spiritual infancy to maturity, becoming vessels through whom the Holy Spirit can work mightily to advance God's kingdom (Ephesians 4:13-15).

Whether you are a new believer seeking to understand the work of the Holy Spirit or a seasoned believer desiring to grow deeper in your walk, *Living By The Spirit* will provide a roadmap to experiencing the abundant life Christ has promised (John 10:10). May this journey lead you into a greater revelation of the Spirit's power, presence, and purpose in your life.

Chapter One

THE HOLY SPIRIT

The study of the Holy Spirit is known in theological terms as Pneumatology, derived from the Greek words pneuma (spirit, breath, or wind) and logos (study, word, or discourse). This area of study is essential for every believer who desires to grow in their relationship with God, as life in the Spirit begins with the Holy Spirit Himself.

THE PERSONHOOD OF THE HOLY SPIRIT

A common misconception about the Holy Spirit is that He is merely an impersonal force or influence rather than a distinct person. However, the clear and unmistakable teaching of Scripture affirms that the Holy Spirit possesses full personality.

One theological definition states, *"A person is that which, when speaking, says 'I'; when spoken to, is called 'thou' (you); and when spoken of, is called 'his' or 'him.'"* (Farr). This understanding is supported by numerous passages in the Bible where personal pronouns are used in relation to the Holy Spirit.

Jesus Himself refers to the Holy Spirit as He rather than it, affirming His personhood. Consider the following passages:

1. **John 14:16-17 (NKJV)** – *"And I will pray the Father, and He will give you another Helper, that He may abide with you forever— the Spirit of truth, whom the world cannot receive, because it neither sees Him nor knows Him; but you know Him, for He dwells with you and will be in you."*

2. **John 15:26 (NKJV)** – *"But when the Helper comes, whom I shall send to you from the Father, the Spirit of truth who proceeds from the Father, He will testify of Me."*

3. **John 16:7-14 (NKJV)** – *"Nevertheless I tell you the truth. It is to your advantage that I go away; for if I do not go away, the Helper will not come to you; but if I depart, I will send Him to you. And when He has come, He will convict the world of sin, and of righteousness, and of judgment: of sin, because they do not believe in Me; of righteousness, because I go to My Father and you see Me no more; of judgment, because the ruler of this world is judged. I still have many things to say to you, but you cannot bear them now. However, when He, the Spirit of truth, has come, He will guide you into all truth; for He will not speak on His own authority, but whatever He hears He will speak; and He will tell you things to*

come. He will glorify Me, for He will take of what is Mine and declare it to you."

THE CHARACTERISTICS OF THE HOLY SPIRIT

The Holy Spirit possesses distinct personal qualities that reveal His divine nature.

1. Knowledge

The Holy Spirit is not an impersonal force but possesses intelligence and understanding. Paul emphasizes this in his letter to the Corinthians:

- **1 Corinthians 2:9-13 (NKJV)** – *"But as it is written: 'Eye has not seen, nor ear heard, nor have entered into the heart of man the things which God has prepared for those who love Him.' But God has revealed them to us through His Spirit. For the Spirit searches all things, yes, the deep things of God. For what man knows the things of a man except the spirit of the man which is in him? Even so no one knows the things of God except the Spirit of God."*

The Spirit possesses the ability to search and reveal deep truths, guiding believers into divine wisdom.

2. Love

The Holy Spirit demonstrates love, another key attribute of personhood.

- **Romans 15:30 (NKJV)** – *"Now I beg you, brethren, through the Lord Jesus Christ, and through the love of the*

Spirit, that you strive together with me in prayers to God for me."

- **2 Timothy 1:7 (NKJV)** – "*For God has not given us a spirit of fear, but of power and of love and of a sound mind.*"

The Spirit's love empowers believers, reassuring them of their divine adoption into the family of God.

3. Will

The Holy Spirit also has a will, as demonstrated in His distribution of spiritual gifts.

- **1 Corinthians 12:11 (NKJV)** – "*But one and the same Spirit works all these things, distributing to each one individually as He wills.*"

This passage confirms that the Spirit actively decides how and to whom spiritual gifts are given, underscoring His sovereign will.

THE HOLY SPIRIT AND THE GODHEAD

The word "*Godhead*" (Gk. *theiótes*) is used in the New Testament and means "*deity, divinity, divine nature or the state of being God.*" God has revealed Himself in the person of the Holy Spirit. He is known as "the spirit of God." Thus, the Holy Spirit is divine:

1. **Acts 17:29 (NKJV)** – "*Therefore, since we are the offspring of God, we ought not to think that the Divine Nature is like gold or silver or stone, something shaped by art and man's devising.*"
2. **Romans 1:20 (NKJV)** – "*For since the creation of the world His invisible attributes are clearly seen, being*

understood by the things that are made, even His eternal power and Godhead, so that they are without excuse."

3. **Colossians 2:9 (NKJV)** – "*For in Him [Christ] dwells all the fullness of the Godhead bodily.*"

These verses affirm that the Holy Spirit is fully God, possessing divine attributes such as eternity, omniscience, omnipotence, and omnipresence.

THE DIVINE ATTRIBUTES OF THE HOLY SPIRIT

Throughout Scripture, the Holy Spirit is revealed to possess divine attributes. He is eternal, omniscient, omnipotent, and omnipresent—meaning that He is without beginning or end, all-knowing, all-powerful, and present everywhere. These attributes confirm that the Holy Spirit is not merely a force or influence but fully God.

1. The Holy Spirit is Eternal

Eternity is an essential characteristic of God, and Scripture affirms that the Holy Spirit is eternal.

*   **Hebrews 9:14 (NKJV)** – "*How much more shall the blood of Christ, who through the eternal Spirit offered Himself without spot to God, cleanse your conscience from dead works to serve the living God?*"

Because the Holy Spirit is eternal, He is not created but exists outside of time. This means that His work in the believer's life is never-ending—He was present in creation, is active in redemption, and will be with believers throughout eternity.

2. The Holy Spirit is Omniscient (All-Knowing)

The Holy Spirit possesses infinite knowledge, searching the deep things of God and revealing divine wisdom to believers.

- **1 Corinthians 2:10-11 (NKJV)** – *"But God has revealed them to us through His Spirit. For the Spirit searches all things, yes, the deep things of God. For what man knows the things of a man except the spirit of the man which is in him? Even so no one knows the things of God except the Spirit of God."*

The Spirit's omniscience enables Him to guide believers into all truth (John 16:13). He knows the mind of God and reveals it to those who seek Him, leading them in righteousness and understanding.

3. The Holy Spirit is Omnipotent (All-Powerful)

The Holy Spirit is the power of God at work in creation, in Christ's ministry, and in the life of every believer.

- **Luke 1:35 (NKJV)** – *"And the angel answered and said to her, 'The Holy Spirit will come upon you, and the power of the Highest will overshadow you; therefore, also, that Holy One who is to be born will be called the Son of God.'"*

The Spirit's omnipotence was evident in the miraculous conception of Jesus and is continually demonstrated through His work in miracles, healings, and spiritual transformation. No power in the universe exceeds the power of the Holy Spirit.

4. The Holy Spirit is Omnipresent (Everywhere at Once)

Unlike a physical being confined to one location, the Holy Spirit is present everywhere at all times.

- **Psalm 139:7-10 (NKJV)** – *"Where can I go from Your Spirit? Or where can I flee from Your presence? If I ascend into heaven, You are there; If I make my bed in hell, behold, You are there. If I take the wings of the morning, And dwell in the uttermost parts of the sea, Even there Your hand shall lead me, And Your right hand shall hold me."*

Because of His omnipresence, the Holy Spirit is always with believers, guiding, convicting, and comforting them no matter where they are.

THE PERSONAL CHARACTERISTICS OF THE HOLY SPIRIT

Beyond His divine attributes, the Holy Spirit possesses personal characteristics that affirm His identity as a person rather than an impersonal force. These include intelligence, emotions, and will.

1. The Holy Spirit Has Intelligence

The Holy Spirit's intelligence is revealed in His ability to teach, reveal truth, and search the depths of God's wisdom.

- **John 14:26 (NKJV)** – *"But the Helper, the Holy Spirit, whom the Father will send in My name, He will teach you all things, and bring to your remembrance all things that I said to you."*
- **Isaiah 40:13-14 (NKJV)** – *"Who has directed the Spirit of the Lord, or as His counselor has taught Him? With*

whom did He take counsel, and who instructed Him, and taught Him in the path of justice? Who taught Him knowledge, and showed Him the way of understanding?"

His role as a teacher and revealer of divine truth showcases His vast intelligence. He instructs believers in the things of God and enables them to comprehend spiritual matters.

2. The Holy Spirit Has Emotions

Unlike an impersonal force, the Holy Spirit experiences emotions such as love and grief.

- **Romans 15:30 (NKJV)** – *"Now I beg you, brethren, through the Lord Jesus Christ, and through the love of the Spirit, that you strive together with me in prayers to God for me."*
- **Ephesians 4:30 (NKJV)** – *"And do not grieve the Holy Spirit of God, by whom you were sealed for the day of redemption."*

These passages reveal that the Spirit expresses love for believers and can experience grief when they sin. His emotions reflect His deep care and desire for holiness in the lives of God's people.

3. The Holy Spirit Has a Will

The Holy Spirit makes decisions, distributes spiritual gifts, and directs believers in their calling.

- **1 Corinthians 12:11 (NKJV)** – *"But one and the same Spirit works all these things, distributing to each one individually as He wills."*

- **Acts 13:2 (NKJV)** – *"As they ministered to the Lord and fasted, the Holy Spirit said, 'Now separate to Me Barnabas and Saul for the work to which I have called them.'"*

His ability to make decisions, distribute gifts, and call individuals into ministry confirms His will and active role in guiding the Church.

The Holy Spirit is more than a force or influence; He is fully God and fully personal. He is eternal, omniscient, omnipotent, and omnipresent, and He actively works in the lives of believers. His intelligence, emotions, and will confirm that He is not an abstract power but a living, divine being.

As we grow in our walk with God, we must learn to recognize and respond to the Holy Spirit's presence and leading. Through Him, we are empowered to live by the Spirit, experience God's truth, and walk in divine power and purpose.

THE WORK OF THE HOLY SPIRIT IN THE BELIEVER

The Holy Spirit's work in a believer's life is vast, touching every aspect of spiritual growth and transformation. Below are 15 essential works of the Holy Spirit that enable believers to live by the Spirit (Galatians 5:16):

1. Regenerates (John 3:5; Titus 3:5)
2. Sanctifies (2 Thessalonians 2:13; 1 Peter 1:2)
3. Frees from sin and death (Romans 8:2)
4. Empowers (Acts 1:8)
5. Strengthens (Ephesians 3:16)
6. Confirms sonship (Romans 8:14, 16)
7. Produces fruit (Galatians 5:22-23)
8. Guides into truth (John 16:13)

9. Brings remembrance (John 14:26)
10. Reveals deep truths (1 Corinthians 2:10)
11. Helps in prayer (Romans 8:26)
12. Inspires worship (John 4:24)
13. Separates for service (Acts 13:2)
14. Quickens the body (Romans 8:11)
15. Distributes spiritual gifts (1 Corinthians 12:7-11)

Conclusion

Understanding the Holy Spirit is crucial for every believer. He is not an abstract force but a divine person actively working in the lives of God's people. He teaches, convicts, empowers, and leads us into a deeper relationship with Christ. As we yield to Him, we experience the fullness of life in the Spirit, walking in victory, power, and purpose.

References
Pardington, George P. Outline Studies In Christian Doctrine. p.291.

Chapter Two

THE SPIRIT OF MAN

INTRODUCTION TO THE SPIRIT OF MAN

The study of humanity and its divine origin is known as *anthropology,* derived from the Greek words *anthropos* (man) and *logos* (study). Biblical anthropology examines mankind's creation, nature, and purpose as designed by God. In Genesis, we find that humanity was created uniquely among all living beings—made in the image and likeness of God and endowed with dominion over the earth.

This chapter will explore the creation of man, the tripartite nature of humanity (spirit, soul, and body), the role of dominion given to mankind, and the creation of woman as a divine counterpart.

THE CREATION OF MAN

Scripture clearly teaches that God intentionally and purposefully created mankind:

- **Genesis 1:26-29 (NKJV)** – *"Then God said, 'Let Us make man in Our image, according to Our likeness; let them have dominion over the fish of the sea, over the birds of the air, and over the cattle, over all the earth and over every creeping thing that creeps on the earth.' So God created man in His own image; in the image of God He created him; male and female He created them. Then God blessed them, and God said to them, 'Be fruitful and multiply; fill the earth and subdue it; have dominion over the fish of the sea, over the birds of the air, and over every living thing that moves on the earth.'"*

MAN IN THE IMAGE AND LIKENESS OF GOD

God's intention for Adam was His intention for the entire human race: to bear His image, reflect His character, and exercise dominion over the earth.

1. **In His Image (tselem)**
   - The Hebrew word *tselem* means *"shadow, phantom, or representative figure."* It denotes resemblance or an image that reflects the original.
   - Just as a shadow represents the shape of a real object, mankind was created to visibly reflect the unseen God.
2. **In His Likeness (demuth)**
   - The Hebrew word *demuth* means "similitude" or "similarity."

- This likeness is not physical but moral, intellectual, and spiritual. Man was created with characteristics that reflect God's nature—love, holiness, righteousness, peace, goodness, kindness, and the ability to commune with Him.

THE ROLE OF DOMINION

God entrusted Adam with rulership over the earth. The Hebrew word used for "dominion" in Genesis 1:26 is *radah,* meaning *"to rule, reign, dominate, subjugate, or prevail."* Humanity was given the responsibility of governing the earth as God's steward.

The psalmist echoes this divine assignment:

- **Psalm 8:3-8 (NKJV)** – *"When I consider Your heavens, the work of Your fingers, the moon and the stars, which You have ordained, what is man that You are mindful of him, and the son of man that You visit him? For You have made him a little lower than the angels, and You have crowned him with glory and honor. You have made him to have dominion over the works of Your hands; You have put all things under his feet, all sheep and oxen—even the beasts of the field, the birds of the air, and the fish of the sea that pass through the paths of the seas."*

The psalmist uses a different Hebrew word for dominion, *mashal,* which means *"to govern or steward."* This confirms that while God retains ownership of the earth, mankind is given the responsibility to manage it.

- **Psalm 115:16 (NKJV)** – *"The heaven, even the heavens, are the Lord's; but the earth He has given to the children of men."*

THE TRIPARTITE NATURE OF MAN

Human beings are created as tripartite beings—comprising spirit, soul, and body.

- **Genesis 2:7 (NKJV)** – *"And the Lord God formed man of the dust of the ground, and breathed into his nostrils the breath of life; and man became a living being."*

1. **Body** (Physical Being) – Formed from the dust of the earth.
2. **Spirit** (God-Breathed Life) – The immortal, God-conscious part of man.
3. **Soul** (Mind, Will, Emotions) – The self-conscious part that processes experiences.

Paul affirms this threefold nature:

- **1 Thessalonians 5:23 (NKJV)** – *"Now may the God of peace Himself sanctify you completely; and may your whole spirit, soul, and body be preserved blameless at the coming of our Lord Jesus Christ."*

The distinction between spirit and soul is also found in:

- **Hebrews 4:12 (NKJV)** – *"For the word of God is living and powerful, and sharper than any two-edged sword, piercing even to the division of soul and spirit, and of joints* *and marrow, and is a discerner of the thoughts and intents of the heart."*

Man is primarily a spirit that possesses a soul and lives in a body. The spirit enables communication with God, the soul governs emotions and intellect, and the body interacts with the physical world.

THE CREATION OF WOMAN

God's creation was not complete with Adam alone. Woman was created as a divine complement to man.

* **Genesis 2:21-23 (NKJV)** – *"And the Lord God caused a deep sleep to fall on Adam, and he slept; and He took one of his ribs, and closed up the flesh in its place. Then the rib which the Lord God had taken from man He made into a woman, and He brought her to the man. And Adam said: 'This is now bone of my bones and flesh of my flesh; she shall be called Woman, because she was taken out of Man.'"*

The Hebrew word for made in Genesis 2:22 is *banah*, meaning *"to build"* or *"skillfully fashion."* This indicates that Eve was intricately formed to fulfill a divine purpose.

The Role of Woman as Helpmate

* **Genesis 2:18 (NKJV)** – *"And the Lord God said, 'It is not good that man should be alone; I will make him a helper comparable to him.'"*

The Hebrew word for helper is *ezer,* meaning *"one who aids or supports."* This does not denote inferiority but divine partnership.

Paul reaffirms the unity between man and woman:

- **1 Corinthians 11:7-9 (NKJV)** – *"For man is not from woman, but woman from man. Nor was man created for the woman, but woman for the man."*

Eve was created to complete Adam, demonstrating God's design for mutual dependence in marriage.

Conclusion

Mankind was created in God's image to reflect His character and exercise dominion over the earth. Adam was given stewardship, not ownership, of creation, and Eve was formed as his divine counterpart.

However, Adam's fall severed his connection to God's image, leading to sin's entrance into the world. This loss necessitated the coming of Jesus Christ, who, as the express image of God (Hebrews 1:3), came to restore mankind to its original purpose.

Key Takeaways

1. Humanity is a tripartite being—spirit, soul, and body.
2. God gave man dominion, but not ownership, over the earth.
3. The woman was created as a complementary partner to man.
4. The loss of God's image through sin was restored through Christ.

As we continue in *Living By the Spirit*, we will explore how believers are restored into the image of Christ and how the Holy Spirit enables us to fulfill God's original purpose for humanity.

Chapter Three

DOMINION AND SALVATION IN CHRIST

THE DIVINE MANDATE: MAN'S DOMINION OVER THE EARTH

From the beginning, God entrusted mankind with dominion over the earth. This mandate was not merely a privilege but a divine responsibility to steward creation in alignment with God's will.

- **Genesis 1:26-28 (NKJV)** – *"Then God said, 'Let Us make man in Our image, according to Our likeness; let them have dominion over the fish of the sea, over the birds of the air, and over the cattle, over all the earth and over every creeping thing that creeps on the earth.' So God created man in His own image; in the image of God He created* *him; male and female He created them. Then God blessed them, and God said to them, 'Be fruitful and multiply; fill the earth and subdue it; have dominion over the fish of the sea, over the birds of the air, and over every living thing that moves on the earth.'"*

The word **dominion** (Heb. *radah*) means *"to rule, reign, or subjugate."* This word suggests that Adam was to exercise authority under God's sovereignty. This dominion was not about exploitation but about **stewardship**—a sacred duty to cultivate, protect, and govern the earth in alignment with divine principles.

The Connection Between Dominion and God's Kingdom

God's ultimate intention was for earth to reflect heaven. Man was created to be **God's representative** on earth, ruling in His image while being subject to His authority. The model for this rulership is seen in Psalm 8:

- **Psalm 8:4-6 (NKJV)** – *"What is man that You are mindful of him, and the son of man that You visit him? For You have made him a little lower than the angels, and You have crowned him with glory and honor. You have made him to have dominion over the works of Your hands; You have put all things under his feet."*

This divine assignment places mankind in a **kingly** position—ruling over God's creation as His delegated authority. However, this dominion was lost through sin, necessitating redemption through Jesus Christ.

THE LOSS OF DOMINION: THE FALL OF MAN

How Adam Lost Authority

Adam's sin in the Garden of Eden resulted in the forfeiture of his dominion. Instead of ruling as God's steward, he became subject to sin, death, and the deception of Satan.

- **Genesis 3:6-7 (NKJV)** – *"So when the woman saw that the tree was good for food, that it was pleasant to the eyes, and a tree desirable to make one wise, she took of its fruit and ate. She also gave to her husband with her, and he ate. Then the eyes of both of them were opened, and they knew that they were naked."*

When Adam disobeyed God, he surrendered his authority to Satan. This is why, in the New Testament, Satan is called "the god of this world."

- **2 Corinthians 4:4 (NKJV)** – *"Whose minds the god of this age has blinded, who do not believe, lest the light of the gospel of the glory of Christ, who is the image of God, should shine on them."*
- **Luke 4:5-6 (NKJV)** – *"Then the devil, taking Him [Jesus] up on a high mountain, showed Him all the kingdoms of the world in a moment of time. And the devil said to Him, 'All this authority I will give You, and their glory; for this has been delivered to me, and I give it to whomever I wish.'"*

Satan's claim over earthly authority was not false; it was a **result of Adam's surrender**. The rulership God originally gave to mankind was usurped by the enemy, leading to a world dominated by sin, corruption, and death.

THE PURPOSE OF SALVATION IN CHRIST: RESTORING DOMINION

Jesus, the Second Adam, Restores Authority

Jesus Christ came to **reclaim the dominion** that Adam lost and restore humanity to its original position of ruling with God. This is why Paul calls Him the "Last Adam."

- **1 Corinthians 15:45-47 (NKJV)** – *"And so it is written, 'The first man Adam became a living being.' The last Adam became a life-giving spirit. However, the spiritual is not first, but the natural, and afterward the spiritual. The first man was of the earth, made of dust; the second Man is the Lord from heaven."*

Where Adam failed, Christ succeeded. Through His perfect obedience, sacrificial death, and victorious resurrection, Jesus **legally reclaimed dominion over the earth** from Satan.

- **Colossians 2:14-15 (NKJV)** – *"Having wiped out the handwriting of requirements that was against us, which was contrary to us. And He has taken it out of the way, having nailed it to the cross. Having disarmed principalities and powers, He made a public spectacle of them, triumphing over them in it."*

Jesus did not come merely to forgive sin—He came to **restore the kingdom** and restore man to his rightful place.

- **Matthew 28:18 (NKJV)** – *"And Jesus came and spoke to them, saying, 'All authority has been given to Me in heaven and on earth.'"*

This declaration signifies a **transfer of authority**. Christ, having defeated Satan, now extends His victory to those who believe in Him.

THE CHURCH'S ROLE IN EXERCISING DOMINION

As believers, we are called to **enforce Christ's victory** and reclaim dominion through His name.

- **Luke 10:19 (NKJV)** – *"Behold, I give you the authority to trample on serpents and scorpions, and over all the power of the enemy, and nothing shall by any means hurt you."*
- **Romans 5:17 (NKJV)** – *"For if by the one man's offense death reigned through the one, much more those who receive abundance of grace and of the gift of righteousness will reign in life through the One, Jesus Christ."*

Through Jesus, **we are restored to a place of rulership,** not by physical conquest but through spiritual authority. This includes:

1. **Spreading the Gospel** – Expanding God's kingdom through evangelism (Matthew 28:19-20).
2. **Walking in Victory** – Living a life free from the power of sin (Romans 6:14).
3. **Enforcing God's Will** – Using prayer and faith to manifest His purposes on earth (Matthew 16:19).

The Church is not called to be passive but to **establish God's kingdom** in every sphere of influence.

THE FUTURE OF DOMINION: THE FULL RESTORATION

While believers currently walk in **spiritual dominion**, the full restoration of the earth will occur when Christ returns.

- **Revelation 11:15 (NKJV)** – *"Then the seventh angel sounded: And there were loud voices in heaven, saying, 'The kingdoms of this world have become the kingdoms of our Lord and of His Christ, and He shall reign forever and ever!'"*
- **Revelation 22:5 (NKJV)** – *"And they shall reign forever and ever."*

Christ's dominion will be **fully realized at the end of time**, and believers will reign with Him eternally. Until then, we are called to walk in the victory of His kingdom on earth.

Conclusion

Key Takeaways

1. Adam was given dominion to rule the earth as God's representative.
2. Sin resulted in the loss of this dominion, transferring authority to Satan.
3. Jesus Christ came to restore dominion, defeating Satan and reclaiming authority.
4. Through Christ, believers now exercise spiritual dominion, enforcing God's kingdom through faith, obedience, and prayer.
5. The full restoration of dominion will occur when Christ establishes His eternal reign.

Dominion and Salvation in Christ

As followers of Christ, we are not just saved to go to heaven—
we are saved to reign on earth as stewards of God's kingdom,
walking in His authority and advancing His divine plan.

Chapter Four

THE FALL OF MAN AND THE FORFEITURE OF DOMINION

INTRODUCTION: THE GREATEST TRAGEDY IN HUMAN HISTORY

The fall of man is one of the most significant events in human history. It marks the moment when mankind lost its divine connection with God, forfeited dominion over the earth, and plunged into sin and death. The temptation in the Garden of Eden was not merely about eating forbidden fruit; it was about rebellion against divine authority, a choice to trust the deceiver rather than the Creator.

This chapter will explore the fall of man, the deception of Satan, the consequences of sin, and the nature of mankind after the fall. Additionally, we will define temptation, analyze Satan's threefold method of temptation, and examine how sin altered humanity's relationship with God.

THE FALL OF MAN: A DETAILED ANALYSIS

Genesis 3:1-7 – The Temptation and Fall

- **Genesis 3:1-7 (NKJV)** – *"Now the serpent was more cunning than any beast of the field which the Lord God had made. And he said to the woman, 'Has God indeed said, "You shall not eat of every tree of the garden"?' And the woman said to the serpent, 'We may eat the fruit of the trees of the garden; but of the fruit of the tree which is in the midst of the garden, God has said, "You shall not eat it, nor shall you touch it, lest you die."' Then the serpent said to the woman, 'You will not surely die. For God knows that in the day you eat of it your eyes will be opened, and you will be like God, knowing good and evil.' So when the woman saw that the tree was good for food, that it was pleasant to the eyes, and a tree desirable to make one wise, she took of its fruit and ate. She also gave to her husband with her, and he ate. Then the eyes of both of them were opened, and they knew that they were naked; and they sewed fig leaves together and made themselves coverings."*

This passage outlines the **progression of temptation and sin** that led to the fall of humanity. It began with a conversation between Eve and the serpent, followed by deception, disobedience, and spiritual death.

THE PROBATION: ADAM'S PERIOD OF TESTING

What is Probation?

God placed Adam in the Garden of Eden, a paradise of beauty, abundance, and divine fellowship. However, Adam was also placed in a state of probation—a period of testing to prove his obedience and loyalty to God.

The Hebrew word for *garden* is **"gan"**, meaning "enclosure." Just as an enclosure is designed to protect and contain, the Garden of Eden was both a place of **pleasure** and a place of **testing**.

- Definition of Probation: A proving or testing period where responsibility is given under a law of duty.
- Dr. Miley states: "Probation is a temporary economy. Its central reality is responsibility for conduct under a law of duty."

God allowed Adam to be tested to reveal the **depth of his character and faithfulness.** Just as manufacturers put their products through **quality assurance tests,** Adam was put through a **spiritual quality test** to determine whether he would obey God in love or choose self-will.

Why Was Testing Necessary?

Though Adam and Eve were created in holiness and righteousness, they still possessed **free will**. God did not create robots; He created beings capable of love, choice, and obedience. For their love and faithfulness to be **validated**, they had to be **tested**.

Even Jesus, the Son of God, **learned obedience through suffering:**

- **Hebrews 5:8 (NKJV)** – "Though He was a Son, yet He learned obedience by the things which He suffered."
- **Hebrews 2:17-18 (NKJV)** – "Therefore, in all things He had to be made like His brethren, that He might be a merciful and faithful High Priest in things pertaining to God, to make propitiation for the sins of the people. For in that He Himself has suffered, being tempted, He is able to aid those who are tempted."

Adam and Eve's probation was necessary because **obedience requires a law of duty**. Their test was simple:

- **Genesis 2:16-17 (NKJV)** – *"And the Lord God commanded the man, saying, 'Of every tree of the garden you may freely eat; but of the tree of the knowledge of good and evil you shall not eat, for in the day that you eat of it you shall surely die.'"*

THE TEMPTATION: SATAN'S DECEPTION

Satan's Method of Temptation in the Garden

The serpent (Satan) was crafty and deceptive, manipulating Eve into questioning God's command. His strategy involved three steps:

1. Satan questioned what God said – *"Has God indeed said…?"* (Genesis 3:1)
2. Satan contradicted God's command – *"You will not surely die."* (Genesis 3:4)

3. Satan promised divine benefits – *"Your eyes will be opened, and you will be like God."* (Genesis 3:5)

Eve saw, desired, and took—a pattern that repeats in every temptation.

WHAT IS TEMPTATION?

Temptation is an enticement to sin—a persuasion to do something contrary to God's will.

- **James 1:14-15 (NKJV)** – *"But each one is tempted when he is drawn away by his own desires and enticed. Then, when desire has conceived, it gives birth to sin; and sin, when it is full-grown, brings forth death."*

Temptation does not necessitate sin—but falling into it does. Jesus was tempted but did not sin (Hebrews 4:15).

Satan's Threefold Method of Temptation

The same threefold temptation used in the Garden of Eden was later used against Jesus and continues today:

- **1 John 2:16 (NKJV)** – *"For all that is in the world—the lust of the flesh, the lust of the eyes, and the pride of life—is not of the Father but is of the world."*

TEMPTATION TYPE	EVE'S TEMPTATION	JESUS' TEMPTATION
Lust of the Flesh	*"Good for food"*	*"Turn stones into bread"*
Lust of the Eyes	*"Pleasant to the eyes"*	*"All the kingdoms of this world"*
Pride of Life	*"Desirable to make one wise"*	*"Throw yourself down from the temple*

Satan tempts through **physical desire, visual appeal, and self-exaltation.**

THE FALL: CONSEQUENCES OF SIN

Adam and Eve's disobedience resulted in devastating consequences:

1. The Image of God was corrupted – They no longer reflected God's holiness.
2. Fear and shame entered the human race – "I heard Your voice, and I was afraid." (Genesis 3:10)
3. Sin and death spread to all mankind – "Through one man's sin, death spread to all men." (Romans 5:12)
4. The environment was cursed – "Cursed is the ground for your sake." (Genesis 3:17)
5. They lost access to the Tree of Life – "He drove out the man." (Genesis 3:24)

Conclusion: The Need for Redemption

Adam's failure resulted in mankind's fallen nature, making redemption necessary. Jesus, the Last Adam, came to restore what was lost.

- **Romans 5:19 (NKJV)** – *"For as by one man's disobedience many were made sinners, so also by one Man's obedience many will be made righteous."*

Through Christ, the dominion lost in the Garden is restored, and believers are empowered to resist temptation and live victoriously.

Chapter Five

BORN OF THE SPIRIT

INTRODUCTION: THE NECESSITY OF SPIRITUAL BIRTH

Jesus Christ declared a profound truth when speaking to Nicodemus, a ruler of the Jews, about salvation:

John 3:3 (NKJV) – *"Most assuredly, I say to you, unless one is born again, he cannot see the kingdom of God."*

This statement was not about physical rebirth but a spiritual transformation—a supernatural work of the Holy Spirit in a believer's life. Being born again or born of the Spirit is the only way a person can enter God's kingdom. It is not a religious practice, a moral improvement, or a personal resolution to do better; rather, it is the divine regeneration of a person's spirit, making them a new creation in Christ.

This chapter will explore what it means to be born of the Spirit, the process of regeneration, the contrast between the old nature and the new nature, and the role of the incorruptible seed in spiritual rebirth.

WHAT DOES IT MEAN TO BE BORN AGAIN?

To be born again (Greek: anōthen – "from above") means to receive new spiritual life from God. This transformation is not the result of human effort but is solely the work of the Holy Spirit.

Jesus explains this to Nicodemus:

- **John 3:5-6 (NKJV)** – *"Most assuredly, I say to you, unless one is born of water and the Spirit, he cannot enter the kingdom of God. That which is born of the flesh is flesh, and that which is born of the Spirit is spirit."*

Here, Jesus differentiates between natural birth (born of the flesh) and spiritual birth (born of the Spirit).

How Does a Person Become Born Again?

A person is born again through faith in Jesus Christ and the work of the Holy Spirit. The process involves:

1. **Hearing the Gospel** – The message of salvation through Jesus Christ. (Romans 10:17)
2. **Conviction by the Holy Spirit** – The Spirit makes a

person aware of their sin and need for salvation. (John
16:8-11)

3. **Repentance and Faith** – Turning away from sin and
believing in Jesus. (Acts 3:19, John 3:16)
4. **Regeneration by the Holy Spirit** – The Spirit imparts
new life to the believer. (Titus 3:5)
5. **Confession of Christ as Lord** – A public declaration of
faith. (Romans 10:9-10)

REGENERATION: THE MIRACLE OF NEW BIRTH

Definition of Regeneration

Regeneration is the supernatural act of God imparting spiritual
life to a person who was spiritually dead.

- **Titus 3:5 (NKJV)** – *"Not by works of righteousness which
we have done, but according to His mercy He saved us,
through the washing of regeneration and renewing of the
Holy Spirit."*

The Greek word for **regeneration** (Gk. *palingenesia*) means
"new birth" or *"rebirth."* It signifies a complete transformation
from spiritual death to spiritual life.

- **2 Corinthians 5:17 (NKJV)** – *"Therefore, if anyone is in
Christ, he is a new creation; old things have passed away;
behold, all things have become new."*

This transformation is instant in the spirit but continues as a
lifelong process in the soul and body through sanctification.

Why Is Regeneration Necessary?

1. **Mankind Is Spiritually Dead** – Because of Adam's sin, all people are born spiritually separated from God.
   - **Ephesians 2:1 (NKJV)** – *"And you He made alive, who were dead in trespasses and sins."*
2. **Human Effort Cannot Produce Spiritual Life** – Good works or religious rituals do not achieve salvation.
   - **John 1:12-13 (NKJV)** – *"But as many as received Him, to them He gave the right to become children of God, to those who believe in His name: who were born, not of blood, nor of the will of the flesh, nor of the will of man, but of God."*
3. **Only the Holy Spirit Can Give Life** – Jesus emphasized that the Spirit is the source of new birth.
   - **John 6:63 (NKJV)** – *"It is the Spirit who gives life; the flesh profits nothing. The words that I speak to you are spirit, and they are life."*

THE INCORRUPTIBLE SEED: THE WORD OF GOD IN SALVATION

What Is the Incorruptible Seed?

The Bible teaches that spiritual birth is produced by the incorruptible seed of God's Word.

- **1 Peter 1:23 (NKJV)** – *"Having been born again, not of corruptible seed but incorruptible, through the word of God which lives and abides forever."*

This incorruptible seed is the eternal Word of God, which brings forth spiritual life in a believer. Just as a physical seed produces life in the natural world, the Word of God implanted in a person's heart produces new spiritual life.

- **James 1:18 (NKJV)** – *"Of His own will He brought us forth by the word of truth, that we might be a kind of firstfruits of His creatures."*

THE NEW NATURE VS. THE OLD NATURE

When a person is born again, they receive a new nature—one that is made in the likeness of Christ. However, they must still contend with their old sinful nature.

1. The Old Nature (Fallen Nature)

Before salvation, every person has a sinful nature inherited from Adam. This nature is rebellious against God and enslaved to sin.

- **Romans 7:18 (NKJV)** – *"For I know that in me (that is, in my flesh) nothing good dwells."*
- **Ephesians 4:22 (NKJV)** – *"That you put off, concerning your former conduct, the old man which grows corrupt according to the deceitful lusts."*

Characteristics of the Old Nature:
  » **Enslaved to sin** *(Romans 6:6)*
  » **Separated from God** *(Isaiah 59:2)*
  » **Produces works of the flesh** *(Galatians 5:19-21)*

2. The New Nature (Spirit-Led Nature)

When a person is born of the Spirit, they receive a new nature that desires righteousness and holiness.

- **Ephesians 4:24 (NKJV)** – *"And that you put on the new man which was created according to God, in true righteousness and holiness."*
- **Colossians 3:10 (NKJV)** – *"And have put on the new man who is renewed in knowledge according to the image of Him who created him."*

Characteristics of the New Nature:
» **Led by the Spirit** *(Romans 8:14)*
» **Desires holiness** *(1 Peter 1:15-16)*
» **Produces fruit of the Spirit** *(Galatians 5:22-23)*

How to Live in the New Nature

1. **Renew Your Mind Daily** – Meditate on God's Word. *(Romans 12:2)*
2. **Walk in the Spirit** – Be led by the Holy Spirit. *(Galatians 5:16)*
3. **Crucify the Flesh** – Deny sinful desires. *(Colossians 3:5)*
4. **Put on Christ** – Live in obedience to God. *(Romans 13:14)*

Conclusion: The Power of Being Born Again

Before the foundation of the world, the Father meticulously designed a plan to redeem humanity from sin and deliver us from the hand of the enemy—this divine plan is salvation. Jesus, the Son of God, beheld the plan and willingly agreed to become the perfect sacrifice to redeem mankind from sin—this is redemption. Through Christ, God was reconciling the world to Himself, restoring the relationship that was broken by sin *(2 Corinthians 5:18)*—this is reconciliation.

To all who believe that the Father sent Jesus as the Savior of the world *(faith)*, He grants the power to become sons (Gk. Teknon—meaning "offspring") of God (John 1:12)—this is sonship. As the Scriptures declare, *"For by grace you have been saved through faith, and that not of yourselves; it is the gift of God, not of works, lest anyone should boast" (Ephesians 2:8-9)*—this is grace, God's unmerited favor.

Through the new birth *(regeneration)*, God removes the guilt and penalty of sin through a legal act of justification, accrediting His righteousness to us—this is imputation. As a result, we become partakers of His divine nature *(2 Peter 1:4)*, indwelt by His Spirit, who leads us as sojourners in this world and keeps us from straying from the path set before us. Jesus declared, *"I am the way, the truth, and the life; no one comes to the Father except through Me" (John 14:6).*

Be born of His Spirit *(John 3:8)*, become a new creation in Christ *(2 Corinthians 5:17)*, and walk in the newness of life *(Romans 6:4)* that He has given to us today.

Being born of the Spirit is the most **transformational experience** in a person's life. It changes their **identity, nature,** and **destiny.**

John 3:7 (NKJV) – *"Do not marvel that I said to you, 'You must be born again.'"*

Every believer is called to walk in the **newness of life**, free from the power of sin and alive to God. This is the foundation of a **Spirit-filled life**, where the believer operates in victory, righteousness, and divine purpose.

Chapter Six

SPIRITUAL GROWTH

WHAT IS SPIRITUAL GROWTH?

Spiritual growth is the ongoing process of maturing in one's relationship with Jesus Christ and becoming more like Him in character, conduct, and faith. It is not an instant transformation but a lifelong journey of deepening our connection with God and aligning our lives with His will.

Two key words define spiritual growth:

1. **Process** – A series of intentional actions or steps taken to achieve a specific goal.
2. **Mature** – Fully developed, reaching a state of completeness and ripeness in character and faith.

Biblical Command to Grow Spiritually

Scripture encourages and commands believers to pursue spiritual growth:

- **2 Peter 3:18 (NKJV)** – *"But grow in the grace and knowledge of our Lord and Savior Jesus Christ. To Him be the glory both now and forever. Amen."*
- **Hebrews 6:1 (NKJV)** – *"Therefore, leaving the discussion of the elementary principles of Christ, let us go on to perfection, not laying again the foundation of repentance from dead works and of faith toward God."*

Spiritual growth is not optional; it is a divine expectation for every believer.

THE GOAL OF SPIRITUAL GROWTH: SPIRITUAL MATURITY

The ultimate goal of spiritual growth is spiritual maturity, which is another term for Christlikeness. A mature Christian exhibits the character of Christ, especially when facing challenges, temptations, and hardships.

Three Key Aspects of Spiritual Maturity

1. It Is the Father's Intent for Us
   - **Matthew 5:48 (AMP)** – *"You, therefore, will be perfect [growing into complete maturity of godliness in mind and character, having reached the proper height of virtue and integrity], as your heavenly Father is perfect."*

- **1 Peter 5:10 (NKJV)** – "But may the God of all grace, who called us to His eternal glory by Christ Jesus, after you have suffered a while, perfect, establish, strengthen, and settle you."
- **Hebrews 13:20-21 (NKJV)** – "Now may the God of peace who brought up our Lord Jesus from the dead, that great Shepherd of the sheep, through the blood of the everlasting covenant, make you complete in every good work to do His will."

2. It Is the Goal of Discipleship
   - **Colossians 1:28 (NIV)** – *"He is the one we proclaim, admonishing and teaching everyone with all wisdom, so that we may present everyone fully mature in Christ."*
   - **Colossians 4:12 (CJB)** – *"Epaphras sends greetings; he is one of you, a slave of the Messiah Yeshua who always agonizes in his prayers on your behalf, praying that you may stand firm, mature, and fully confident as you devote yourselves completely to God's will."*

3. It Should Be a Personal Goal for Every Believer
   - **Philippians 3:14-15 (NASB)** – *"I press on toward the goal for the prize of the upward call of God in Christ Jesus. Let us, therefore, as many as are perfect, have this attitude."*
   - **Hebrews 5:14 (NLT)** – *"Solid food is for those who are mature, who have trained themselves to recognize the difference between right and wrong and then do what is right."*

Spiritual maturity is not about being flawless but about being **complete, whole,** and **fully developed** in our relationship with God.

TÉKNON: THE CONCEPT OF OFFSPRING IN SCRIPTURE

Throughout the New Testament, the terms *"child"* and *"son"* are often used interchangeably. However, this does not always capture the full depth of what the biblical authors intended to communicate. This has led to misinterpretations of key theological concepts, such as adoption in Christ. A crucial distinction must be made between spiritual growth levels and one's identity as an offspring of God.

One of the most commonly used Greek words for "child" is **téknon**, which simply means **offspring**. Unlike other Greek terms that signify stages of maturity, téknon does not denote spiritual growth or development. Instead, it refers to someone who is a **descendant by birth**, an offspring of a parent.

Téknon is used figuratively to describe anyone who is fully dependent on their heavenly Father, willing to trust and submit to Him in faith. This dependence on God is a prerequisite for spiritual transformation—before we can grow into Christlikeness, we must first embrace a childlike reliance on Him.

Scriptural References to Téknon

1. **Téknon as Physical Offspring**
   - **Matthew 3:9 (NKJV)** – *"And do not think to say to yourselves, 'We have Abraham as our father.' For I say to you that God is able to raise up children (téknon – offspring) to Abraham from these stones."*
   - This passage illustrates that téknon primarily signifies biological or ancestral lineage, not necessarily maturity or development.
2. **Téknon as Those Who Receive Christ**
   - **John 1:12 (NKJV)** – *"But as many as received Him,*

to them He gave the right to become children (téknon – offspring) of God, to those who believe in His name."
- Here, téknon is used to describe those who have been **born into the family of God through faith** in Jesus Christ. However, this is only the starting point of their spiritual journey.

3. **Téknon as Heirs in Christ**
   - **Romans 8:16-17 (NKJV)** – *"The Spirit Himself bears witness with our spirit that we are children (téknon – offspring) of God, and if children, then heirs—heirs of God and joint-heirs with Christ, if indeed we suffer with Him, that we may also be glorified together."*
   - This passage highlights that being God's offspring **entitles** believers to an inheritance, but it does not imply spiritual maturity.

Téknon and the Spiritual Growth Process

Unlike words like népios (infant), paidíon (young child), and huiós (mature son), téknon is not simply a stage of development. Rather, it represents a foundational identity that denotes belonging to God's family. All believers begin their journey as téknon—children of God by faith—but are called to grow into huiós—spiritually mature sons and daughters who embody Christ's character and authority.

Key Takeaway

While téknon establishes one's identity as a child of God, it does not reflect spiritual development or growth. Every believer is a child of God, but spiritual maturity necessitates growth beyond being merely an offspring. This progression will be discussed further in the exploration of **spiritual adoption (huiothesia)**—the placement of mature sons into their divine inheritance.

THE PROCESS OF SPIRITUAL GROWTH

Spiritual maturity is a journey, not a destination. Like natural life progresses from infancy to adulthood, spiritual growth follows a similar pattern. The Bible describes different stages of spiritual development using specific Greek words:

1. **Népios** (Infant or Babe in Christ) – A newborn believer who is dependent, unskilled, and in need of guidance. It can also refer to immaturity and being untrained.
   - **1 Corinthians 3:1** – *"I could not speak to you as to spiritual people but as to carnal, as to babes in Christ."*
   - **1 Peter 2:2** – *"As newborn babes, desire the pure milk of the word, that you may grow thereby."*
2. **Paidíon** (Young Child, Learner) – A growing believer who is still learning but has some understanding.
   - **Matthew 18:3** – *"Unless you are converted and become as little children, you will by no means enter the kingdom of heaven."*
3. **Huiós** (Mature Son, Spiritually Led) – A believer who is fully mature, walking in the Spirit, and entrusted with responsibility.
   - **Romans 8:14** – *"For as many as are led by the Spirit of God, these are sons of God."*
4. **Pater** (Father, Spiritual Mentor) – A believer who has grown to maturity and is helping others grow in Christ.
   - **1 John 2:13-14** – *"I am writing to you, fathers, because you know Him who has been from the beginning."*

Six Key Factors in Spiritual Growth

1. **The Word of God** – The primary source of growth.
   - **2 Timothy 3:16-17** – *"All Scripture is given by inspiration of God, and is profitable for doctrine, for reproof, for correction, for instruction in righteousness, that the man of God may be complete."*
2. **Prayer and Communion with God** – Strengthens our spiritual life.
   - **Jude 1:20** – *"But you, beloved, building yourselves up on your most holy faith, praying in the Holy Spirit."*
3. **God's Discipline (Chastening)** – Helps correct and refine us.
   - **Hebrews 12:6-7** – *"For whom the Lord loves He chastens, and scourges every son whom He receives."*
4. **Fivefold Ministry** (Apostles, Prophets, Evangelists, Pastors, Teachers) – Helps equip believers for maturity.
   - **Ephesians 4:11-13** – *"He gave some to be apostles, prophets, evangelists, pastors, and teachers, for the equipping of the saints, for the work of ministry, for the edifying of the body of Christ, till we all come to the unity of the faith, to a perfect man."*
5. **Speaking the Truth in Love** – Strengthens believers in their walk.
   - **Ephesians 4:15** – *"Speaking the truth in love, may grow up in all things into Him who is the head—Christ."*
6. **Trials and Suffering** – Produces perseverance and maturity.
   - **1 Peter 5:10** – *"After you have suffered for a little while, the God of all grace, who called you to His eternal glory in Christ, will Himself perfect, confirm, strengthen, and establish you."*

SONSHIP - The Teknon (Offspring) of God - Born of His Spirit

immature untrained · babe Nepios

under instructors · child Paidon

mature son Huios · can handle the father's business

father Pater · prepares sons for inheritance leaves legacy

HUIOTHESIA—THE CALL TO MATURE SONSHIP

Throughout Scripture, the theme of sonship is central to the believer's journey with God. While many recognize the privilege of being called children of God, fewer understand the deeper reality of huiothesia, the biblical doctrine of adoption. In Western culture, adoption is generally understood as the process of legally taking in an unrelated child and granting them familial status. However, biblical adoption in Greco-Roman culture carried a far deeper meaning, one that speaks profoundly to our spiritual maturity and Kingdom inheritance.

The Meaning of Huiothesia

The Greek word **"huiothesia"** is a compound term formed from **"huios,"** meaning **"mature son,"** and **"thesis,"** meaning **"placement"** or **"positioning."** Thus, huiothesia literally means **"the placing of a son"** or **"sonship by adoption."** This concept appears prominently in the writings of Paul:

- *"For you have not received a spirit of bondage again to fear, but you have received* **the Spirit of adoption**

(huiothesia), *by whom we cry, 'Abba, Father.'"* (Romans 8:15)

- *"To redeem those who were under the law, that we might receive the* **adoption (huiothesia) as sons**.*"* (Galatians 4:5)
- *"Having predestined us to* **adoption (huiothesia) as sons** *by Jesus Christ to Himself, according to the good pleasure of His will."* (Ephesians 1:5)

These verses reveal that adoption in the biblical sense **is not about rescuing an orphaned child** but **the intentional placement of a person into full sonship, with all the rights, privileges, and inheritance of a mature heir.**

CONTRASTING HUIOTHESIA WITH WESTERN ADOPTION

To fully appreciate the biblical meaning of huiothesia, we must distinguish it from the modern Western concept of adoption. The following table outlines the major differences:

Aspect	Biblical Adoption (Huiothesia)	Western Adoption
Definition	The legal placement of a person (often an adult) into sonship, granting full rights and inheritance.	The legal process of placing a child into a new family, often due to abandonment, orphanhood, or inability of biological parents to care for them.
Age of Adoptee	Typically an adult or mature child who could inherit and continue the family legacy.	Usually an infant or young child who needs care and a home.

Aspect	Biblical Adoption (Huiothesia)	Western Adoption
Purpose	To bestow the full rights of inheritance and authority within a family, often to secure a successor.	To provide care, love, and a family for a child who lacks one.
Status Before Adoption	The adoptee may have already been part of the household but without full inheritance rights (e.g., a servant or an unrecognized son).	The adoptee is typically unrelated to the adoptive family before the process.
Legal & Social Impact	A full change in legal status, where the adoptee receives the father's name, inheritance, and position of honor. Their past debts and obligations are erased.	A change in legal status, but often without the same cultural emphasis on inheritance and legal succession.
Spiritual Implication	A believer, though born again as a child of God (teknon), is positioned as a mature son (huios) with full Kingdom authority and inheritance.	Often focuses on care and relationship rather than the idea of being positioned for rulership and inheritance.

This distinction is critical. **Huiothesia is not simply about being included in God's family—it is about being positioned for Kingdom rulership, authority, and inheritance.**

FROM CHILDREN (TEKNON) TO SONS (HUIOS)

The New Testament makes a distinction between children (teknon - offspring) and sons (huios - mature sons). While all believers are born again as children of God, not all live as mature sons who understand and walk in their divine inheritance.

Paul explains this progression in Galatians 4:1-7:

> *"Now I say that the heir, as long as he is a child (nepios), does not differ at all from a slave, though he is master of all, but is under guardians and stewards until the time appointed by the father."* (Galatians 4:1-2)

In this passage, the child (nepios), though an heir by birth, cannot yet access his inheritance because of immaturity. He must come into a stage of sonship (huios) before he can be entrusted with the responsibilities of an heir.

Signs of a Mature Son (Huios)

1. **Led by the Spirit** – *"For as many as are led by the Spirit of God, these are sons (huios) of God."* (Romans 8:14)
2. **Lives in Intimacy with the Father** – *"You have received the Spirit of adoption (huiothesia) by whom we cry, 'Abba, Father.'"* (Romans 8:15)
3. **Walks in Inheritance and Authority** – *"And if children, then heirs—heirs of God and joint heirs with Christ."* (Romans 8:17)
4. **Displays the Character of Christ** – *"For whom He foreknew, He also predestined to be conformed to the image of His Son (huios)."* (Romans 8:29)

This means that spiritual maturity is not about how long someone has been "born again," but about how deeply they are submitted to the Holy Spirit and walking in their Kingdom identity.

THE FINAL ADOPTION: FULL REDEMPTION IN CHRIST

Paul also speaks of a future fulfillment of huiothesia:

> *"And not only that, but we also who have the firstfruits of the Spirit, even we ourselves groan within ourselves, eagerly waiting for the adoption (huiothesia), the redemption of our body."* (Romans 8:23)

This verse reveals that while we are already positioned as sons, the fullness of our adoption will be realized when we receive our glorified bodies. In other words, huiothesia is both a present reality and a future promise.

Walking in Your Sonship

To truly embrace huiothesia, we must shift our mindset:

- From spiritual infancy (passivity, insecurity, and dependence)
- To spiritual sonship (maturity, authority, and co-heirship with Christ)

As sons, we are called to rule, govern, and bring the Kingdom of God into the earth (Romans 5:17, Revelation 5:10). The Holy Spirit is constantly leading us into greater maturity so that we can walk in the fullness of our inheritance in Christ.

Key Takeaways

1. Huiothesia is not just about being accepted into God's family—it's about being positioned for inheritance and responsibility.
2. Spiritual sonship is a process of maturing from being a child of God (teknon) to a fully developed son (huios).
3. True sons are led by the Spirit, walk in intimacy with the Father, and exercise Kingdom authority.
4. The ultimate fulfillment of our adoption will come when we receive our glorified bodies at Christ's return.

As believers, our goal is not just to be saved—but to be mature sons, walking in the fullness of our divine inheritance, reflecting the image of Christ, and advancing His Kingdom on earth. This is the power of huiothesia—the call to sonship.

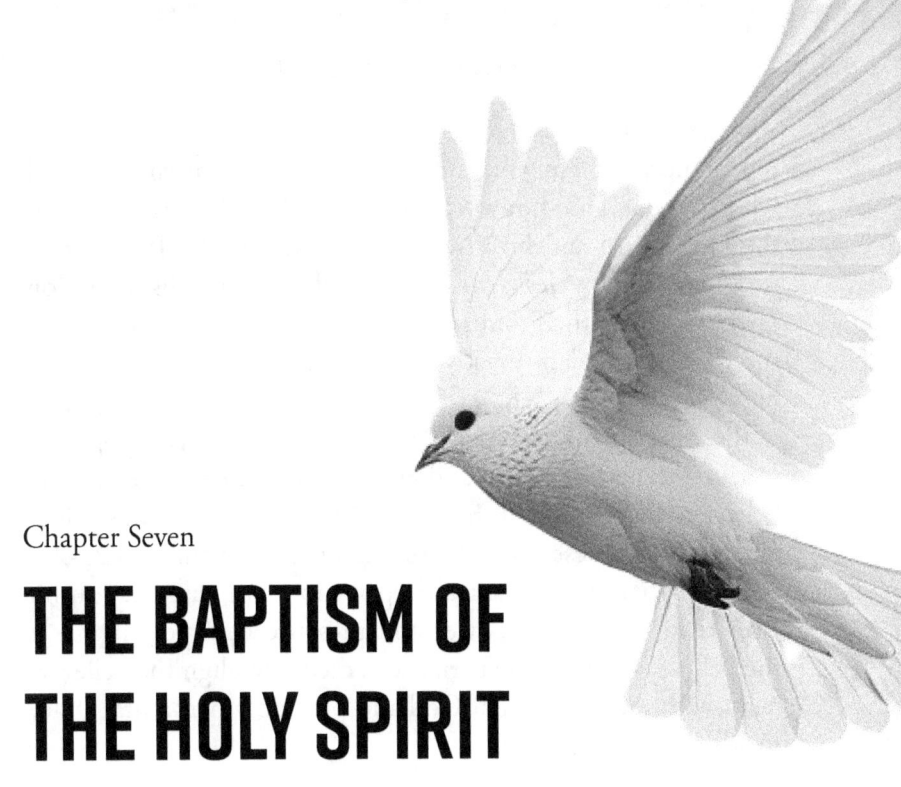

Chapter Seven

THE BAPTISM OF THE HOLY SPIRIT

THE BAPTISM OF THE HOLY SPIRIT

One of the most vital doctrines of the Christian faith is the baptism of the Holy Spirit. This divine endowment is a distinct and subsequent experience to salvation, empowering believers for effective witness and victorious Christian living (Matthew 3:11; Luke 24:49; Acts 1:8). It is a gift from God, intended to equip the believer with supernatural power to fulfill the Great Commission and live in continual communion with Him.

The Promise of the Father

John the Baptist prophesied the coming baptism of the Holy Spirit, declaring: "I indeed baptize you with water unto repentance, but He who is coming after me is mightier than I, whose sandals I am not worthy to carry. He will baptize you with the Holy Spirit and fire" (Matthew 3:11, NKJV). This promise was reiterated by Jesus to His disciples before His ascension: "Behold, I send the Promise of My Father upon you; but tarry in the city of Jerusalem until you are endued with power from on high" (Luke 24:49, NKJV).

The baptism of the Holy Spirit is not merely an optional spiritual experience but a divine empowerment that enables believers to live out their faith with boldness, operate in spiritual gifts, and manifest the fruit of the Spirit (Galatians 5:22-23). It is an invitation to enter a deeper, more intimate relationship with God, where His power and presence become tangible in the believer's life. This experience is meant to align the believer's heart with the purposes of God and provide supernatural ability to advance His kingdom.

A DISTINCT AND SUBSEQUENT EXPERIENCE

The New Testament consistently presents the baptism of the Holy Spirit as an experience that follows salvation. When Jesus spoke to the Samaritan woman at the well, He differentiated between the "well of water springing up into everlasting life" (salvation) and "rivers of living water" (the Holy Spirit) (John 4:14; John 7:38-39). The imagery of a well versus rivers signifies that salvation secures eternal life, but the baptism of the Holy Spirit unleashes a continuous flow of divine power and anointing in the believer's life.

This distinction is further confirmed in the Book of Acts:

1. **The Samaritans' Experience (Acts 8:5-17)** – Philip preached Christ to the people of Samaria, and they

believed and were baptized in water. Yet, it was only when Peter and John laid hands on them that they received the Holy Spirit.

2. **The Ephesian Disciples (Acts 19:1-7)** – Paul encountered disciples in Ephesus who had believed in Jesus but had not yet received the Holy Spirit. After baptizing them in the name of Jesus, he laid hands on them, and they received the Holy Spirit, evidenced by speaking in tongues and prophesying.

3. **The Apostle Paul's Experience (Acts 9:1-17)** – Saul encountered Jesus on the road to Damascus and was converted. However, it was only when Ananias laid hands on him that he was filled with the Holy Spirit.

These accounts clearly show that the baptism of the Holy Spirit is a distinct work of grace following salvation, meant to equip believers with supernatural power. This divine encounter is essential for unlocking the fullness of God's call in a believer's life, as it enhances spiritual sensitivity, deepens intercessory prayer, and empowers one to operate in the supernatural dimension of faith.

THE EVIDENCE OF THE BAPTISM: SPEAKING IN TONGUES

The initial evidence of being baptized in the Holy Spirit is speaking in tongues as the Spirit gives utterance (Acts 2:4; Acts 10:44-46; Acts 19:6). On the Day of Pentecost, when the Holy Spirit was poured out, **"they were all filled with the Holy Spirit and began to speak with other tongues, as the Spirit gave them utterance"** (Acts 2:4, NKJV). Similarly, when Peter preached to the Gentiles in the house of Cornelius, **"they heard them speak with tongues and magnify God"** (Acts 10:46, NKJV).

Speaking in tongues serves multiple purposes in the life of a believer:

- It is a supernatural sign of the Holy Spirit's infilling.
- It serves as a prayer language for direct communion with God (1 Corinthians 14:2).
- It builds up the believer's faith and spiritual strength (Jude 1:20).
- It is a gateway to operating in other spiritual gifts (1 Corinthians 12:8-10).
- It enables deeper intercessory prayer, allowing the Holy Spirit to pray through the believer in alignment with God's perfect will (Romans 8:26-27).

POWER FOR WITNESS AND SERVICE

The baptism of the Holy Spirit is not just for personal edification but for empowerment to witness (Acts 1:8). Jesus commanded His disciples to wait in Jerusalem until they received this power, knowing they would need divine enablement to carry out the Great Commission. The outpouring of the Spirit transformed the disciples from fearful followers into bold proclaimers of the gospel, leading to the rapid expansion of the early Church.

Alton Garrison aptly states, *"The baptism in the Holy Spirit provides the believer with an empowering for witness and to live a life pleasing to God"* (Garrison, 2009). This divine empowerment enables believers to speak with boldness, operate in miraculous signs, and be led by the Spirit in every area of life, confirming the gospel with power.

RECEIVING THE BAPTISM OF THE HOLY SPIRIT

Every believer is entitled to and should earnestly seek this divine experience (Ephesians 5:18). Jesus assured that the Father delights in giving the Holy Spirit to those who ask (Luke 11:13). The steps to receiving the baptism of the Holy Spirit include:

1. **Repentance and Faith in Jesus Christ** – The Holy Spirit is given only to those who have been born again (John 3:3-8).
2. **Desiring and Asking for the Holy Spirit** – Jesus promised, "Ask, and it will be given to you; seek, and you will find; knock, and it will be opened to you" (Luke 11:9-13).
3. **Yielding to the Holy Spirit** – The believer must surrender in faith, allowing the Spirit to take full control (Acts 2:4).
4. **Laying on of Hands** – In many biblical instances, the Holy Spirit was received through the laying on of hands (Acts 8:17; Acts 19:6).
5. **Expecting and Acting in Faith** – Receiving the Holy Spirit requires faith, just as receiving salvation does. The believer must step out in faith and speak as the Spirit enables them (Acts 2:4).

Conclusion

The baptism of the Holy Spirit is a powerful, life-changing experience that God desires for every believer. It is not just for the apostles or early Christians but is available today for all who hunger for more of God. It is the key to living a victorious Christian life, fulfilling the mission of Christ, and operating in the supernatural power of God.

May every believer passionately seek this gift, walk in the fullness of the Spirit, and boldly declare the gospel to the ends of the earth.

References:
- Garrison, A. (2009). *Acts 2: The Church Reborn.* Springfield, MO: Gospel Publishing House.
- Holy Bible, New King James Version (NKJV).
- Horton, S. M. (1996). *What the Bible Says About the Holy Spirit.* Springfield, MO: Gospel Publishing House.

Chapter Eight

THE FRUIT OF THE SPIRIT

The fruit of the Spirit is the evidence of a life that is fully surrendered to God and led by the Holy Spirit. It is not merely a set of virtues to strive for, but rather the natural byproduct of a heart that has been transformed by divine influence. As believers yield to the Spirit, they cultivate a Christlike character that overcomes the power of sin, fosters unity in the body of Christ, and enables them to walk in continuous fellowship with God.

THE CONTRAST BETWEEN FLESH AND SPIRIT

The apostle Paul presents a stark contrast between the works of the flesh and the fruit of the Spirit in Galatians 5. The works of the flesh signify a life governed by sinful desires, while the fruit of the Spirit represents a life under divine control, reflecting God's nature and righteousness.

Galatians 5:22-23 (KJV) states: *"But the fruit of the Spirit is love, joy, peace, longsuffering, gentleness, goodness, faith, meekness, temperance: against such there is no law."*

Paul lists the works of the flesh in Galatians 5:16-21, describing behaviors such as immorality, idolatry, jealousy, anger, and divisions. These sinful tendencies hinder the believer's spiritual growth and disrupt their relationship with God. Paul warns that those who habitually engage in such practices will not inherit the kingdom of God.

THE NINEFOLD FRUIT OF THE SPIRIT

The fruit of the Spirit is singular, yet it consists of nine attributes that collectively shape the believer's character. These virtues are interconnected, working together to produce a life that reflects the love and holiness of God.

1. **Love (Agape)** – Selfless, unconditional love that seeks the highest good of others. It is the foundation of Christian character and reflects God's nature (1 Corinthians 13:4-8; John 15:13).
2. **Joy (Chara)** – A deep, abiding sense of gladness that stems from knowing and trusting God, independent of circumstances (Nehemiah 8:10; John 15:11; James 1:2-3).
3. **Peace (Eirene/Shalom)** – Inner tranquility and wholeness that result from reconciliation with God, leading to stability in all aspects of life (Romans 5:1; Philippians 4:7; Isaiah 26:3).
4. **Longsuffering (Makrothumia)** – Patient endurance in trials, displaying a steadfast attitude in the face of opposition or offense (Colossians 3:12; Ephesians 4:2).

5. **Gentleness (Chrestotes)** – A disposition of kindness, moral integrity, and helpfulness that reflects God's character (Titus 3:4; 2 Timothy 2:24).

6. **Goodness (Agathosune)** – Active benevolence and righteousness, which includes standing up against evil and working toward justice (Romans 15:14; Ephesians 5:9).

7. **Faith (Pistis)** – Steadfast trust in God, reliability, and unwavering loyalty to His truth (Hebrews 11:6; Matthew 25:21).

8. **Meekness (Prautes)** – Humility and controlled strength that enables believers to submit to God's will and treat others with grace (Matthew 5:5; James 1:21; Galatians 6:1).

9. **Temperance (Enkrateia)** – Self-control and mastery over desires, impulses, and emotions, especially in resisting sin (1 Corinthians 9:24-27; 2 Peter 1:5-6).

CULTIVATING THE FRUIT OF THE SPIRIT

The fruit of the Spirit is not produced by human effort but by abiding in Christ. Jesus declared, "Abide in me, and I in you. As the branch cannot bear fruit of itself, except it abide in the vine; no more can ye, except ye abide in me" (John 15:4, KJV). True spiritual fruitfulness results from intimacy with Christ and complete dependence on the Holy Spirit.

Practical Ways to Cultivate the Fruit of the Spirit:

- Daily surrender to the Holy Spirit (Romans 8:13-14)
- Consistent prayer and communion with God (1 Thessalonians 5:17)

- Renewing the mind through God's Word (Romans 12:2)
- Obedience to God's commands (John 14:15)
- Fellowship with other believers (Hebrews 10:24-25)
- Practicing forgiveness and love (Ephesians 4:32)
- Developing spiritual disciplines like fasting and worship (Matthew 6:16-18)
- Serving others with humility and compassion (Philippians 2:3-4)

THE NECESSITY OF THE FRUIT OF THE SPIRIT

While spiritual gifts empower believers for ministry, the fruit of the Spirit qualifies them for service. A believer can possess spiritual gifts yet lack godly character, leading to spiritual downfall. Jesus emphasized the importance of fruitfulness, saying, "By their fruits, ye shall know them" (Matthew 7:16). Without the fruit of the Spirit, a believer's witness is compromised, and their ministry effectiveness is diminished.

The fruit of the Spirit is essential because it:

- Demonstrates Christlike character (Romans 8:29)
- Distinguishes true believers (Matthew 7:20)
- Brings glory to God (John 15:8)
- Enables effective ministry (1 Corinthians 13:1-3)
- Strengthens spiritual endurance (James 1:2-4)
- Ensures victory over sin (Galatians 5:16-18)
- Reflects the transformation of a renewed mind (Ephesians 4:22-24)

Fruitfulness and Spiritual Maturity

Spiritual maturity is directly linked to the production of the fruit of the Spirit. A mature believer exhibits increasing levels of love, joy, peace, and self-control in daily life. As the believer grows in Christ, these virtues become more evident, influencing their decisions, interactions, and attitudes.

Additionally, the fruit of the Spirit is a key indicator of spiritual health. Jesus said in John 15:8, *"Herein is my Father glorified, that ye bear much fruit; so shall ye be my disciples."* **Bearing spiritual fruit is a sign of true discipleship and spiritual maturity.**

Conclusion

The fruit of the Spirit is the mark of a life that has been transformed by the power of God. It is the evidence that a believer is walking in step with the Holy Spirit, manifesting the love, righteousness, and holiness of God. As we yield to the Spirit daily, He produces within us a character that reflects the very nature of Christ. This transformation is not instantaneous but rather a lifelong journey of growth, maturity, and sanctification.

May every believer strive to cultivate the fruit of the Spirit, living a life that honors God and impacts the world for His kingdom. By allowing the Spirit to work in us, we become true representatives of Christ, displaying His love and grace to a lost and dying world.

References:

- Horton, S. M. (1996). *What the Bible Says About the Holy Spirit.* Springfield, MO: Gospel Publishing House.
- Bridges, J. (2008). *The Pursuit of Holiness.* Colorado Springs, CO: NavPress.
- Tozer, A. W. (1991). *The Root of the Righteous.* Camp Hill, PA: Christian Publications.
- Murray, A. (1895). *The Spirit of Christ.* New York, NY: Anson D. F. Randolph & Co.

Chapter Nine

GIFTS OF THE SPIRIT

THE GIFTS OF THE SPIRIT

Spiritual gifts are divine enablements bestowed upon believers by the Holy Spirit to equip them for service, edification, and the advancement of God's kingdom. These gifts are not natural talents or acquired skills but supernatural manifestations that empower the body of Christ to function effectively in ministry. The apostle Paul introduces the subject of spiritual gifts in 1 Corinthians 12:1-11, stating:

"Now concerning spiritual gifts, brethren, I would not have you ignorant... Now there are diversities of gifts, but the same Spirit. And there are differences of administrations, but the

same Lord. And there are diversities of operations, but it is the same God which worketh all in all. But the manifestation of the Spirit is given to every man to profit withal" (1 Corinthians 12:1, 4-7, KJV).

Understanding Spiritual Gifts

The Greek term pneumatika charismata refers to spiritual gifts or spiritual grace gifts. These gifts are supernatural in nature and given to believers as the Holy Spirit wills. They are vital for strengthening the church, confirming God's Word, and equipping the saints for effective ministry (Mark 16:17-20, John 14:12, Hebrews 2:1-4).

Dr. C. Peter Wagner states, "Ignorance of spiritual gifts may be a chief cause of retarded church growth today." Hence, it is essential for believers to understand and operate in their spiritual gifts.

THE DIVINE PURPOSE OF SPIRITUAL GIFTS

Spiritual gifts serve several essential purposes:

- They build and strengthen the church (Ephesians 4:12-13).
- They confirm the preaching of the gospel through signs and wonders (Mark 16:20).
- They enable believers to live a Spirit-empowered life (Acts 1:8).
- They help unify the body of Christ (1 Corinthians 12:12-13).
- They prepare believers for effective ministry (2 Timothy 3:17).

Key Truths About Spiritual Gifts

1. We should not be ignorant of spiritual gifts (1 Corinthians 12:1). Understanding them is crucial for spiritual maturity.
2. We should not neglect our spiritual gifts (1 Timothy 4:14).
3. We should stir up the gifts within us (2 Timothy 1:6).
4. Spiritual gifts are supernatural, not natural talents.
5. They originate from the Holy Spirit.
6. The Holy Spirit distributes these gifts as He wills.
7. Their purpose is to confirm God's Word and empower believers (Mark 16:17-20, John 14:12, Hebrews 2:1-4).
8. Spiritual gifts differ from pagan supernatural experiences. The Corinthians were previously led astray by idol worship, but spiritual gifts operate through the Holy Spirit.
9. Two criteria for evaluating spiritual gifts:
   • No one speaking by the Spirit of God calls Jesus accursed.
   • No one can confess Jesus as Lord except by the Holy Spirit (1 Corinthians 12:3).
10. Spiritual gifts manifest the power of God.
11. They are given to every believer to build up the church (1 Corinthians 14:26).
12. They must operate in love; otherwise, they are meaningless (1 Corinthians 13:1-3).
13. Spiritual gifts can be misused or counterfeited (Matthew 7:22-23).
14. Believers should desire spiritual gifts (1 Corinthians 12:31, 14:1).
15. Gifts often operate in combination. For example, miracles and healing frequently work together.

CATEGORIES OF SPIRITUAL GIFTS

To better understand these gifts, they can be categorized into three groups:

1. Revelation Gifts (gifts that reveal something)
   - Word of Wisdom
   - Word of Knowledge
   - Discerning of Spirits
2. Power Gifts (gifts that do something)
   - Gift of Faith
   - Gifts of Healing
   - Working of Miracles
3. Utterance Gifts (gifts that say something)
   - Prophecy
   - Diverse Kinds of Tongues
   - Interpretation of Tongues

The Gifts Explained

1. Word of Wisdom

A supernatural revelation of divine purpose and the mind of God concerning the future. Example: Noah was warned of the coming flood and instructed to build the ark (Genesis 6:13-18). Other examples include Joseph interpreting Pharaoh's dreams (Genesis 41) and Agabus predicting a famine (Acts 11:28).

2. Word of Knowledge

A supernatural revelation of specific facts in the mind of God about present or past events. Example: Jesus told the Samaritan woman about her five husbands (John 4:18), and Peter exposed Ananias and Sapphira's deceit (Acts 5:1-10).

3. Discerning of Spirits

The supernatural ability to distinguish between divine, demonic, and human spirits. Example: Paul discerned the spirit of divination in the slave girl (Acts 16:16-18).

4. Gift of Faith

Supernatural trust in God that results in miracles. Example: Daniel in the lion's den (Daniel 6), Elijah praying for drought and rain (1 Kings 17-18).

5. Gifts of Healing

The supernatural ability to heal sickness without natural means. Example: Peter healing the lame man at the temple gate (Acts 3:1-10).

6. Working of Miracles

A supernatural intervention in the ordinary course of nature. Example: Moses parting the Red Sea (Exodus 14), Jesus feeding the 5,000 (Luke 9:10-17).

7. Gift of Prophecy

A supernatural utterance that edifies, exhorts, and comforts (1 Corinthians 14:3). Example: Agabus prophesying Paul's imprisonment (Acts 21:10-11).

8. Divers Kinds of Tongues

Speaking in a language unknown to the speaker, often for prayer or public edification. Example: The Day of Pentecost (Acts 2:4), Cornelius' household speaking in tongues (Acts 10:44-46).

9. Interpretation of Tongues

The supernatural ability to interpret a message given in tongues. This gift ensures the congregation benefits from messages spoken in tongues (1 Corinthians 14:13).

Additional Spiritual Gifts

Other gifts mentioned in the New Testament include:

- Helps, Administration (1 Corinthians 12:28)
- Service, Teaching, Giving, Leadership, Mercy, Hospitality (Romans 12:6-8)
- Apostles, Prophets, Evangelists, Pastors, Teachers (Ephesians 4:11-13)

Dr. C. Peter Wagner also includes voluntary poverty, celibacy, intercession, and martyrdom as spiritual gifts.

The Importance of Spiritual Gifts in Living by the Spirit

Spiritual gifts are essential for living by the Spirit. They empower believers to minister effectively, strengthen the church, and confirm the gospel with signs and wonders. However, spiritual gifts must be exercised in love and humility. The fruit of the Spirit shapes a believer's character, while the gifts of the Spirit enable them to operate in divine power.

Conclusion

The gifts of the Spirit are divine empowerments given to believers for the edification of the church and the expansion of God's kingdom. Understanding and using these gifts properly enables believers to live by the Spirit, operate in God's power, and bear fruit for His glory.

References:
- Wagner, C. P. (1994). *Your Spiritual Gifts Can Help Your Church Grow.* Ventura, CA: Regal Books.
- Horton, S. M. (1996). *What the Bible Says About the Holy Spirit.* Springfield, MO: Gospel Publishing House.

Chapter Ten

SPIRITUAL WARFARE

The Spiritual Warfare

Spiritual warfare is an integral aspect of the believer's walk in the Spirit. It must be understood and embraced, as it influences every facet of our spiritual growth, obedience to God, and engagement with the kingdom of darkness. Scripture is clear that we fight not against flesh and blood but against spiritual forces that oppose God's will and work.

UNDERSTANDING SPIRITUAL WARFARE

Two primary passages in the New Testament highlight the reality of spiritual warfare:

1. **2 Corinthians 10:3-6** – *"For though we walk in the flesh, we do not war after the flesh: (for the weapons of our warfare are not carnal, but mighty through God to the pulling down of strongholds;) casting down imaginations, and every high thing that exalteth itself against the knowledge of God, and bringing into captivity every thought to the obedience of Christ; and having in a readiness to revenge all disobedience, when your obedience is fulfilled."*
2. **Ephesians 6:10-18** – *"Finally, my brethren, be strong in the Lord, and in the power of His might. Put on the whole armor of God, that ye may be able to stand against the wiles of the devil. For we wrestle not against flesh and blood, but against principalities, against powers, against the rulers of the darkness of this world, against spiritual wickedness in high places..."*

The Reality of the Spiritual Battle

The believer is engaged in an unseen but real conflict. The enemy, Satan, along with his demonic forces, actively seeks to hinder our progress in Christ. Paul admonishes Timothy to fight "the good fight of faith" (1 Timothy 6:12) and to endure hardships as a good soldier of Christ (2 Timothy 2:3). Jesus Himself warned that those who endure to the end shall be saved (Matthew 10:22; Revelation 2:10).

Key Biblical Truths About Spiritual Warfare:

1. Believers are more than conquerors through Christ (**Romans 8:37**).
2. Faith is the key to overcoming the world (1 John 5:4-5).
3. God has given us all things pertaining to life and godliness (2 Peter 1:3).

WHAT IS SPIRITUAL WARFARE?

Spiritual warfare is the ongoing conflict of resisting our sinful nature and actively engaging against the powers of darkness. It is a struggle to live in obedience to God so that our lives mirror the image of Christ. Victory in this battle requires:

1. Presenting our bodies as living sacrifices, holy and acceptable to God (Romans 12:1).
2. Nonconformity to the world's system (Romans 12:2).
3. Transformation by the renewing of our minds (Romans 12:2).

Our Enemy: Understanding the Opposition

1. Satan and fallen angels – Lucifer and his angels rebelled against God and were cast down from heaven (Revelation 12:7-10).
2. Demons – Spirits that seek to oppress, deceive, and possess.
3. The Flesh – Our carnal nature that opposes the Spirit (Galatians 5:16-17).
4. The World System – A society that operates independently of God (1 John 2:15-17).

Jesus identified Satan's mission in John 10:10:

1. To steal – Satan wants to rob us of God's blessings and purposes.
2. To kill – He seeks to physically and spiritually destroy lives.
3. To destroy – His ultimate goal is to separate us from God.

The Enemy's Tactics

1. **Deception** – He masquerades as an angel of light (2 Corinthians 11:14).
2. **Temptation** – Uses our fleshly desires against us.
3. **Opposition and Persecution** – Uses trials to instill fear and doubt.
4. **Strongholds** – False beliefs, pride, and rebellious thoughts that resist God's truth.
5. **False Teachers and Doctrines** – Infiltrates the church with heresy (Matthew 7:15; 2 Timothy 4:3-4).

Equipping for Battle: Our Divine Weapons

Paul instructs believers to put on the whole armor of God (Ephesians 6:10-18):

1. **The Belt of Truth** – Standing on God's Word.
2. **The Breastplate of Righteousness** – Living in holiness.
3. **The Shoes of the Gospel of Peace** – Readiness to share the gospel.
4. **The Shield of Faith** – Protection from the enemy's attacks.
5. **The Helmet of Salvation** – Guarding the mind against deception.
6. **The Sword of the Spirit** – The Word of God as our offensive weapon.
7. **Prayer and Intercession** – Engaging in continual prayer.

Other Mighty Weapons of Warfare

1. **The Name of Jesus** – A powerful weapon against the enemy (Philippians 2:9-11).

2. **The Blood of Jesus** – Overcoming power (Revelation 12:11).
3. **Praise and Worship** – Silencing the enemy (Psalm 8:2).
4. **Fasting and Prayer** – Deepening spiritual strength (Matthew 17:21).
5. **The Anointing** – Breaking yokes and removing burdens (Isaiah 10:27).
6. **Testimony of Overcomers** – Declaring God's faithfulness (Revelation 12:11).
7. **Love and Righteous Living** – A lifestyle that defeats darkness (1 John 4:18).

Deliverance and Casting Out Demons

Casting out demons is a kingdom mandate:

- Jesus cast out demons by the Spirit of God (Matthew 12:27-28).
- Believers have been given authority to do the same (Mark 16:17).
- The early church actively engaged in deliverance (Acts 16:16-18).

BIBLICAL EXAMPLES OF SPIRITUAL WARFARE

The Bible is filled with examples of spiritual warfare, demonstrating how God's people engaged in battle against spiritual forces and the schemes of the enemy. Here are several key examples:

1. The Fall of Lucifer (Isaiah 14:12-15, Ezekiel 28:12-19, Revelation 12:7-9)

Lucifer, once a mighty angel, rebelled against God due to pride and was cast out of heaven along with a third of the angels who followed him. This marked the beginning of the spiritual conflict between God and Satan.

2. The Temptation of Eve (Genesis 3:1-7)

Satan, in the form of a serpent, deceived Eve into disobeying God, introducing sin into the world. This deception continues today as the enemy seeks to distort God's truth.

3. Job's Spiritual Battle (Job 1-2)

Satan challenged Job's faith, seeking to destroy him through loss, sickness, and suffering. However, Job remained faithful, and God restored him, proving that faithfulness leads to victory in spiritual warfare.

4. Daniel's Warfare in Prayer (Daniel 10:10-14)

Daniel fasted and prayed for 21 days, and an angel revealed that his prayer was delayed due to resistance from the "Prince of Persia" (a demonic principality). This highlights the reality of spiritual battles in the unseen realm.

5. Jesus' Temptation in the Wilderness (Matthew 4:1-11)

Satan attempted to tempt Jesus through physical desires, pride, and power. Jesus resisted by declaring the Word of God, demonstrating how believers must use Scripture to combat spiritual attacks.

6. Peter's Denial (Luke 22:31-32)

Jesus warned Peter that Satan sought to "sift him like wheat." This reveals how the enemy desires to weaken believers, but intercession and faith allow them to stand firm.

7. Paul's Thorn in the Flesh (2 Corinthians 12:7-10)

Paul described a "messenger of Satan" sent to torment him. God allowed this trial to keep Paul humble and dependent on divine strength, showing that sometimes spiritual warfare involves enduring trials while trusting in God's grace.

8. The Possessed Man at Gadara (Mark 5:1-20)
Jesus encountered a man possessed by a legion of demons. He commanded the demons to leave, and the man was delivered, demonstrating the power of Christ over demonic forces.

9. The Battle Between Michael and Satan (Jude 1:9, Revelation 12:7-9)

Michael the archangel contended with Satan over the body of Moses, showing the reality of angelic warfare. Revelation 12 describes Michael and his angels fighting against Satan, reinforcing the theme of ongoing cosmic conflict.

Examples of Spiritual Warfare in the Early Church

The early church was no stranger to spiritual warfare. The apostles and early believers encountered significant opposition from demonic forces, false teachings, persecution, and trials. Here are some key examples:

1. Ananias and Sapphira (Acts 5:1-11)

Satan influenced Ananias and Sapphira to lie to the Holy Spirit about their offering. Their immediate judgment demonstrated that spiritual deception within the church is a serious issue.

2. The Persecution of the Apostles (Acts 4-5)

The Pharisaic leaders attempted to silence Peter and John through imprisonment and threats. However, they preached boldly by the power of the Holy Spirit, demonstrating that faithfulness in the face of persecution is a crucial aspect of spiritual warfare.

3. Simon the Sorcerer (Acts 8:9-24)

Simon, a magician, tried to purchase the power of the Holy Spirit. Peter rebuked him, revealing the spiritual conflict between God's power and false miracles.

4. Paul and the Slave Girl with a Spirit of Divination (Acts 16:16-18)

A girl possessed by a demon followed Paul, proclaiming the truth but doing so in a deceitful manner. Paul casts the demon out, angering her owners and showing that spiritual warfare requires confronting demonic influences in society.

5. The Seven Sons of Sceva (Acts 19:13-16)

These Judaean exorcists attempted to cast out demons in the name of Jesus without true authority. The demons overpowered them, illustrating that spiritual warfare requires a genuine relationship with Christ.

6. The Riot in Ephesus (Acts 19:23-41)

The spread of the gospel threatened the local idol-making industry, leading to a violent uproar against Paul and his companions. This shows how spiritual warfare extends to cultural and economic strongholds.

7. Paul's Shipwreck and the Snakebite (Acts 27-28)

Paul faced repeated trials, including a violent storm and a venomous snake bite. Yet, God preserved him, proving that spiritual warfare often involves overcoming life-threatening obstacles.

8. False Teachings in the Church (Galatians 1:6-9, 1 Timothy 4:1-2, 2 Peter 2:1-3)

The early church battled heresies, such as legalism, Gnosticism, and false prophecies. Paul and other apostles consistently warned against false teachers who distorted the gospel.

9. The Martyrdom of Stephen (Acts 7:54-60)

Stephen, full of the Holy Spirit, was stoned to death after boldly proclaiming Christ. His death marked the beginning of severe persecution against the church, demonstrating that spiritual warfare often results in suffering for righteousness.

10. John's Exile to Patmos (Revelation 1:9)

John was exiled for his faith but received the revelation of Jesus Christ, proving that even in suffering, spiritual warfare leads to divine victory.

These biblical and early church examples of spiritual warfare illustrate that the struggle against spiritual forces is continuous. As believers, we are called to stay alert, stand firm in our faith, utilize the full armor of God (Ephesians 6:10-18), and walk in the authority granted to us by Christ (Luke 10:19). Through prayer, the Word, fasting, and obedience, we can overcome every attack from the enemy and expand God's kingdom on earth.

PAUL'S EXAMPLE OF SPIRITUAL WARFARE (EXPOUNDED)

Paul and the Slave Girl with a Spirit of Divination (Acts 16:16-18)

One of the most compelling examples of spiritual warfare in the early church is the encounter between the Apostle Paul and a slave girl who was possessed by a spirit of divination in the city of Philippi. This event demonstrates the clash between the kingdom of God and demonic forces that sought to manipulate and deceive people.

Context: Paul's Mission in Philippi

Paul, along with Silas, Timothy, and Luke, was on a missionary journey when they arrived in Philippi, a major city in the Roman colony of Macedonia. This was the first recorded time the gospel was preached in Europe.

- Paul had received a vision known as the Macedonian Call (Acts 16:9-10), in which a man pleaded, "Come over to Macedonia and help us."
- Obeying this vision, Paul and his team traveled to Philippi, where they began to preach the gospel.

- They first encountered Lydia, a wealthy merchant of purple cloth, who became a believer along with her household after hearing Paul's message (Acts 16:13-15).

After this, they faced a direct confrontation with a demonic spirit operating through a young slave girl.

The Slave Girl and the Spirit of Divination

"And it came to pass, as we went to prayer, a certain damsel possessed with a spirit of divination met us, which brought her masters much gain by soothsaying: The same followed Paul and us, and cried, saying, 'These men are the servants of the most high God, which shew unto us the way of salvation.' And this did she many days. But Paul, being grieved, turned and said to the spirit, 'I command thee in the name of Jesus Christ to come out of her.' And he came out the same hour" (Acts 16:16-18 KJV).

Key Observations:

1. She was a slave girl – The girl was under the control of her masters, who exploited her supernatural abilities for financial gain.
2. She had a spirit of divination – The Greek phrase used for "spirit of divination" is *pneuma Pythōna,* meaning a python spirit. This term was associated with the Oracle of Delphi, a famous prophetic shrine in ancient Greece, where a priestess (Pythia) would utter messages supposedly from Apollo.
3. She was a fortune teller – The girl practiced soothsaying, a form of fortune-telling or divination, which was common in pagan cultures.

87

4. She followed Paul for many days – She persistently followed Paul and his team, proclaiming, "These men are servants of the Most High God!"
5. Paul cast out the spirit in Jesus' name – Paul, filled with the Holy Spirit, discerned the demonic influence and commanded the spirit to leave the girl.

The Nature of the Spiritual Warfare

This was not merely a physical encounter but a spiritual battle in which the kingdom of darkness sought to interfere with the work of God.

Why Was This a Spiritual Attack?

1. The demon spoke truth with deceptive intent
   - The slave girl's words seemed accurate: Paul and his team were, indeed, servants of the Most High God and were preaching salvation. However, Satan often mixes truth with deception to manipulate people.
   - If Paul had accepted her words, people might have associated the gospel with demonic divination, corrupting the purity of Christ's message.
2. It was a strategy of Satan to bring confusion
   - By allowing a demon-possessed girl to proclaim their identity, Satan could make it seem like Paul and his team were operating under the same supernatural power as the pagan diviners of Philippi.
   - This would discredit the gospel and confuse the people.
3. The spirit resisted being cast out

- Paul tolerated this for many days, indicating that this was a persistent spiritual assault.
- The fact that Paul had to command the spirit in the name of Jesus to leave proves that the demon had an entrenched hold on the girl.

The Consequences of the Deliverance

When Paul cast out the spirit, the girl lost her ability to tell fortunes, enraging her masters who had been making a profit from her demonic influence.

> *"And when her masters saw that the hope of their gains was gone, they caught Paul and Silas, and drew them into the marketplace unto the rulers, and brought them to the magistrates, saying, 'These men, being Jews, do exceedingly trouble our city, and teach customs, which are not lawful for us to receive, neither to observe, being Romans.' And the multitude rose up together against them: and the magistrates rent off their clothes, and commanded to beat them. And when they had laid many stripes upon them, they cast them into prison, charging the jailer to keep them safely"* (Acts 16:19-24 KJV).

Key Results of the Spiritual Warfare:

1. The girl's deliverance caused economic loss
   - The slave owners lost their income source and were furious.
   - This demonstrates that spiritual warfare is not only about casting out demons but also about dismantling systems of oppression.

2. Paul and Silas were persecuted for delivering the girl
   - They were falsely accused of promoting unlawful customs.
   - They were severely beaten and imprisoned without trial.
   - This shows that spiritual warfare often leads to persecution.
3. God used their imprisonment for His glory
   - While in prison, Paul and Silas prayed and worshiped (Acts 16:25).
   - An earthquake shook the prison, breaking their chains and leading to the salvation of the Philippian jailer and his household (Acts 16:26-34).
   - This shows that victory in spiritual warfare results in the advancement of God's kingdom.

LESSONS FOR BELIEVERS TODAY

1. Discern the Spirit Behind a Message
   - Not every "truth" spoken about God is inspired by the Holy Spirit.
   - Even Satan quotes Scripture (Matthew 4:6), but he does so to deceive.
   - Spiritual discernment is needed to recognize when truth is being manipulated for deception.
2. Boldly Confront the Enemy
   - Paul tolerated the demonic interference for many days but ultimately took authority in Jesus' name.
   - Believers must not tolerate demonic oppression— we have been given power over unclean spirits (Luke 10:19).

3. Deliverance May Have Consequences
   - Casting out demons often disrupts the enemy's agenda, which may bring persecution.
   - Many people and systems benefit from oppression (just as the slave girl's owners did).
   - Expect opposition when engaging in spiritual warfare.
4. Worship Is a Weapon in Spiritual Warfare
   - Even after being beaten and imprisoned, Paul and Silas worshiped.
   - Their worship triggered a divine intervention—an earthquake that set them free!
   - Praise silences the enemy (Psalm 8:2).
5. Spiritual Warfare Leads to Kingdom Expansion
   - The deliverance of one girl led to an entire family being saved (the jailer's household).
   - When we engage in spiritual warfare, we help set captives free and expand God's kingdom.

The story of Paul and the slave girl in Philippi is a powerful example of spiritual warfare. It reveals how Satan seeks to infiltrate the church, manipulate truth, and hinder the gospel. Yet, Paul overcame the attack through spiritual discernment, boldness, and the authority of Jesus' name.

This encounter also emphasizes the cost of engaging in spiritual warfare—persecution, opposition, and suffering—but ultimately shows that God's power prevails, setting captives free and advancing the kingdom of God.

Believers today must remain vigilant, bold in their authority, and persistent in prayer and worship, knowing that victory is assured through Jesus Christ.

THE CALL TO OVERCOME

Victory in spiritual warfare is the hallmark of an overcomer. John writes:

> *"For whatsoever is born of God overcometh the world: and this is the victory that overcometh the world, even our faith"* (1 John 5:4).

The book of Revelation lists nine rewards for overcomers:

1. Access to the Tree of Life (Revelation 2:7).
2. A Crown of Life (Revelation 2:10).
3. Hidden Manna (Revelation 2:17).
4. A New Name on a White Stone (Revelation 2:17).
5. Authority Over Nations (Revelation 2:26).
6. Clothed in White Garments (Revelation 3:5).
7. Name Retained in the Book of Life (Revelation 3:5).
8. Made a Pillar in God's Temple (Revelation 3:12).
9. Seated with Christ on His Throne (Revelation 3:21).

Spiritual warfare is not an option—it is a reality that every believer must engage in to live victoriously in Christ. Through the power of the Holy Spirit, the authority of God's Word, and the application of divine weapons, we can resist the enemy and advance God's kingdom. By standing firm in faith, embracing holiness, and remaining steadfast in prayer, we overcome the adversary and walk in the fullness of God's calling.

Chapter Eleven

SPIRITUAL HABITS: CULTIVATING A LIFE LED BY THE SPIRIT

SPIRITUAL HABITS: CULTIVATING A LIFE LED BY THE SPIRIT

The Christian journey is not merely about believing in Christ; it is about forming a lifestyle that reflects His character and teachings. Our previous lesson on spiritual warfare emphasized the necessity of resisting the enemy and standing firm in faith. However, the battle is not just about opposition but also about building a life of holiness and spiritual discipline. A life change does not happen by accident—it requires intentional spiritual habits that shape our daily walk with God.

The Importance of Spiritual Habits

Spiritual habits are consistent, intentional practices that draw believers closer to God, shape their character, and equip them for a victorious life in the Spirit. The Apostle Paul urges believers to live a consecrated life:

> Romans 12:1-2 (NIV): *"Therefore, I urge you, brothers and sisters, in view of God's mercy, to offer your bodies as a living sacrifice, holy and pleasing to God—this is your true and proper worship. Do not conform to the pattern of this world, but be transformed by the renewing of your mind. Then you will be able to test and approve what God's will is—His good, pleasing and perfect will."*

A consecrated lifestyle—one that is set apart for God—requires commitment. Just as athletes train to discipline their bodies, believers must train themselves in godliness through spiritual habits.

THE FORMULA FOR BUILDING SPIRITUAL HABITS

Devotion = Desire + Determination + Discipline

1. **Desire** – A deep longing and yearning for God that fuels spiritual pursuit and intimacy with Him. The Psalmist likened this desire to a deer panting for water, expressing an intense need for God's presence (Psalm 42:1-2). Jesus reinforced this principle, teaching that prioritizing the Kingdom of God above all else leads to divine provision and fulfillment (Matthew 6:33). This desire compels believers to seek God daily, fostering an unshakable devotion and dependence on Him.

2. **Determination** – A firm decision to seek spiritual growth with unwavering commitment and perseverance. It involves setting one's focus on the things of God,

refusing to be swayed by distractions, and pressing forward despite obstacles (Colossians 3:1-4, Philippians 3:13-14). Determination fuels consistency in prayer, Bible study, and acts of service, ensuring that spiritual disciplines become deeply rooted habits rather than fleeting intentions.

3. **Discipline** – The intentional practice of training oneself in godliness through consistent habits that foster spiritual maturity and obedience to Christ (1 Timothy 4:7-8). This includes the regular exercise of prayer, fasting, studying the Word, and maintaining a life of holiness, ensuring that one's faith is not only professed but actively lived out in daily decisions and actions.

SPIRITUAL HABITS THAT TRANSFORM LIVES

The Bible presents several key habits that believers should cultivate. These habits foster intimacy with God, strengthen faith, and develop Christlike character.

1. Worship: Living in Reverence to God

Worship is not just an event; it is a lifestyle. It is the posture of the heart that acknowledges God's worthiness.

John 4:23-24 (NIV): *"Yet a time is coming and has now come when the true worshipers will worship the Father in the Spirit and in truth, for they are the kind of worshipers the Father seeks."*

Worship involves:

- Singing (Psalm 95:1-2)
- Bowing in reverence (Psalm 95:6)
- Offering our lives (Romans 12:1)

2. Praise: Declaring God's Greatness

Praise is an outward expression of gratitude and joy in God. It is a weapon in spiritual warfare (Psalm 149:6-9) and a key to breakthroughs (Acts 16:25-26).

Forms of Praise:

- Shouting (Psalm 47:1)
- Clapping (Psalm 47:1)
- Dancing (Psalm 149:3)
- Lifting Hands (Psalm 63:4)
- Singing New Songs (Psalm 96:1)
- Playing Instruments (Psalm 150:3-5)

3. Prayer: Communing with God

Prayer is a direct line of communication with God, fostering dependence and intimacy.

> Colossians 4:2 (NIV): *"Devote yourselves to prayer, being watchful and thankful."*

Jesus modeled a life of prayer, often retreating for communion with the Father (Luke 5:16). The early church also emphasized prayer (Acts 2:42), proving its necessity.

Prayer Habits:

- Personal prayer (Matthew 6:6)
- Intercessory prayer (1 Timothy 2:1)
- Corporate prayer (Acts 12:5)

4. Watching: Spiritual Alertness

The Bible repeatedly calls for believers to watch and pray (Matthew 26:41). Spiritual vigilance prevents temptation and deception.

> 1 Peter 5:8 (NIV): *"Be alert and of sober mind. Your enemy the devil prowls around like a roaring lion looking for someone to devour."*

5. Word Intake: Feeding on the Scriptures

The Bible is the source of truth that guides believers (Psalm 119:105). Without regular Bible reading and meditation, spiritual growth stagnates.

> 2 Timothy 2:15 (KJV): *"Study to shew thyself approved unto God, a workman that needeth not to be ashamed, rightly dividing the word of truth."*

Methods of Word Intake:

- Reading (Joshua 1:8)
- Studying (2 Timothy 3:16-17)
- Meditation (Psalm 1:2-3)
- Memorization (Psalm 119:11)

6. Word Confession: Speaking God's Truth

The words we speak shape our reality. Faith-filled confession aligns our lives with God's promises.

Proverbs 18:21 (NIV): *"The tongue has the power of life and death, and those who love it will eat its fruit."*

Confessing God's Word:

- Declaring His promises (2 Corinthians 1:20)
- Overcoming fear (Isaiah 41:10)
- Affirming identity in Christ (2 Corinthians 5:17)

Conclusion

Building spiritual habits is essential for living by the Spirit. They strengthen faith, deepen intimacy with God, and equip believers for victorious living. Developing these habits requires desire, determination, and discipline, leading to a consecrated lifestyle.

By embracing these habits daily, believers experience growth, victory, and the fullness of God's purpose in their lives.

References:
- Holy Bible, New International Version (NIV)
- Foster, R. J. (2018). *Celebration of Discipline: The Path to Spiritual Growth*. HarperOne.
- Whitney, D. S. (2014). *Spiritual Disciplines for the Christian Life*. NavPress.

Chapter Twelve

SPIRITUAL APOSTASY: THE PERIL OF FALLING AWAY

SPIRITUAL APOSTASY: THE PERIL OF FALLING AWAY

The journey of faith is not only about drawing near to God but also about remaining steadfast in Him. Throughout Scripture, we find strong warnings about spiritual apostasy, which is the act of turning away from God and returning to a life of unbelief. This final chapter explores the concept of apostasy, its biblical foundations, the dangers it presents to believers striving to live by the Spirit, and how to safeguard our faith.

Defining Spiritual Apostasy

The term apostasy is derived from the Greek word *apostasia,* meaning *"abandonment, defection, departure, revolt, or rebellion."*

In a biblical context, it refers to a deliberate falling away from faith in Christ. Apostasy is the opposite of conversion; it is a deconversion, where a person who once walked in faith chooses to reject Christ and the salvation they once received.

Apostasy is different from backsliding. While backsliding refers to a temporary period of spiritual decline or sinfulness from which one can repent and return to God, apostasy is a full rejection of the faith. The Bible repeatedly warns about apostasy, demonstrating that it is not merely a theoretical concern but a real and present danger for those who fail to guard their faith.

SCRIPTURAL WARNINGS AGAINST APOSTASY

1. The Possibility of Falling Away

The debate over whether a believer can lose their salvation has persisted for centuries. One of the primary doctrines in this discussion is "Once Saved, Always Saved" (Eternal Security), which suggests that once a person is truly saved, they can never fall away. This doctrine is rooted in John 10:28-29:

> *"I give them eternal life, and they shall never perish; no one will snatch them out of my hand. My Father, who has given them to me, is greater than all; no one can snatch them out of my Father's hand."* (NIV)

While this passage assures believers of God's keeping power, it does not imply that a person cannot choose to walk away from God. The responsibility of remaining in Christ is emphasized throughout the New Testament.

2. Key Scriptures Warning of Apostasy

The Bible contains multiple warnings about the dangers of apostasy:

- **Hebrews 6:4-6** – "For in the case of those who have once been enlightened and have tasted of the heavenly gift and have been made partakers of the Holy Spirit, and have tasted the good word of God and the powers of the age to come, and then have fallen away, it is impossible to renew them again to repentance, since they again crucify to themselves the Son of God and put Him to open shame."
- **2 Peter 2:20-22** – "If they have escaped the corruption of the world by knowing our Lord and Savior Jesus Christ and are again entangled in it and are overcome, they are worse off at the end than they were at the beginning."
- **1 Timothy 4:1** – "Now the Spirit expressly says that in later times some will depart from the faith by devoting themselves to deceitful spirits and teachings of demons."
- **Hebrews 3:12** – "Take care, brothers, lest there be in any of you an evil, unbelieving heart, leading you to fall away from the living God."
- **John 15:6** – "If anyone does not abide in me, he is thrown away like a branch and withers; and the branches are gathered, thrown into the fire, and burned."

These passages emphasize that salvation requires continual faithfulness and that turning away from Christ carries serious consequences.

NEW TESTAMENT EXAMPLES OF APOSTASY

The Bible provides numerous examples of individuals and groups who fell away from their faith:

- Judas Iscariot (Acts 1:25) – He "fell by transgression" and forfeited his apostleship.
- Demas (2 Timothy 4:10) – Left Paul "because he loved this present world."
- Hymenaeus and Alexander (1 Timothy 1:18-20) – Suffered spiritual shipwreck by rejecting the faith.
- Ananias and Sapphira (Acts 5:1-11) – Lied to the Holy Spirit and suffered divine judgment.

These examples remind us that spiritual failure is possible, even for those who once walked closely with God.

The Gradual Steps Toward Apostasy

Apostasy is rarely an instant event; rather, it happens in gradual stages:

1. **Spiritual Neglect** – A failure to take God's Word seriously (Mark 1:15, Hebrews 2:1-3).
2. **Drifting from Christ** – A slow departure from devotion to Jesus (Hebrews 4:16, 7:25).
3. **Compromise with Sin** – Tolerating sin rather than rejecting it (1 Corinthians 6:9-10, Hebrews 3:13).
4. **Hardening of the Heart** – Ignoring the conviction of the Holy Spirit (Hebrews 3:7-11, Ephesians 4:30).
5. **Total Departure from the Faith** – A full renunciation of Christ and salvation (Hebrews 10:26, Hebrews 6:4-6).

The Dangers of Apostasy

The Bible speaks of grave consequences for those who persist in apostasy:

- Loss of Eternal Life (John 15:6, Hebrews 10:26-31)
- Reprobation – Becoming "void of judgment" and unable to return (Romans 1:28, Hebrews 6:4-6).
- Eternal Separation from God (Matthew 7:21-23, Revelation 3:5).

How to Guard Against Apostasy

The Bible provides believers with specific strategies to protect themselves from falling away:

1. **Watch and Pray** – "Watch and pray, lest you enter into temptation." (Matthew 26:41)
2. **Hold Fast to the Faith** – "Holding faith with a pure conscience." (1 Timothy 1:19)
3. **Take Heed** – "Let him who thinks he stands take heed lest he fall." (1 Corinthians 10:12)
4. **Be Rooted in Christ** – "Make your calling and election sure." (2 Peter 1:10)
5. **Stay in Fellowship with Believers** – "Encourage one another daily." (Hebrews 3:13)
6. **Remain in God's Word** – "Let the Word of Christ dwell in you richly." (Colossians 3:16)
7. **Live a Life of Holiness** – "Be holy, for I am holy." (1 Peter 1:16)

Conclusion: The Call to Endurance

Apostasy is not an inevitable fate; it is a conscious decision to turn away from God. The believer's call is to endure to the end (Matthew 24:13). Faithfulness to Christ requires daily commitment, vigilance, and reliance on the Holy Spirit.

The words of Paul summarize the believer's resolve:

"I have fought the good fight, I have finished the race, I have kept the faith." (2 Timothy 4:7-8, NKJV)

May we all strive to remain faithful, standing firm in the Spirit until the end.

Chapter Thirteen

BENEFITS OF LIVING BY THE SPIRIT

The Benefits of Living by the Spirit

The Christian life is not merely about rules, doctrines, or religious traditions—it is about an intimate, dynamic relationship with God through His Holy Spirit. Living by the Spirit is the essence of true Christianity, as it enables believers to walk in divine wisdom, power, and righteousness. It is through the Spirit that we experience transformation, divine insight, and the supernatural ability to fulfill God's purpose in our lives. This chapter explores the manifold benefits of living by the Spirit, supported by Scripture and illustrated by biblical figures who exemplified Spirit-led lives. By examining these benefits, we uncover how the Spirit's presence in our daily walk empowers us to live victoriously, overcome obstacles, and grow into the fullness of our divine calling.

Living By The Spirit

THE GUIDANCE OF THE HOLY SPIRIT

One of the most profound benefits of living by the Spirit is divine guidance. The Holy Spirit leads believers into truth, convicts them of sin, and directs their paths (John 16:13). When we yield to the Spirit, we can discern God's will and make choices that align with His divine purposes. Through prayer, the Word, and sensitivity to the Spirit, believers receive clarity in decision-making, protection from deception, and alignment with God's perfect will.

Biblical Example: Philip and the Ethiopian Eunuch

Philip, one of the early church deacons, was directed by the Holy Spirit to encounter an Ethiopian eunuch. In Acts 8:29, "The Spirit told Philip, 'Go to that chariot and stay near it.'" Because Philip obeyed, he was able to share the Gospel, leading to the eunuch's baptism. This divine appointment demonstrates how the Spirit orchestrates events when we are attuned to His leading. When we live by the Spirit, we position ourselves for supernatural encounters that not only bless us but also bring others into the kingdom of God.

SPIRITUAL TRANSFORMATION AND HOLINESS

The Holy Spirit sanctifies believers, shaping them into the image of Christ. Living by the Spirit produces the fruit of the Spirit—love, joy, peace, patience, kindness, goodness, faithfulness, gentleness, and self-control (Galatians 5:22-23). These virtues distinguish Spirit-led believers and enable them to live in holiness and righteousness. A transformed life reflects God's character and serves as a witness to the world of His power and grace.

106

Biblical Example: Peter's Transformation

Before Pentecost, Peter was impulsive and fearful, even denying Christ three times (Luke 22:61-62). However, after receiving the Holy Spirit (Acts 2), Peter was transformed into a bold preacher of the Gospel. He fearlessly proclaimed Christ before thousands and performed miracles, showcasing the power of a Spirit-led life. His transformation exemplifies the Spirit's ability to change a person from weakness to strength, from fear to boldness, and from instability to unwavering faith.

SUPERNATURAL POWER AND MIRACLES

A life yielded to the Spirit is marked by divine power. Jesus declared, "You will receive power when the Holy Spirit comes on you" (Acts 1:8). This power is not for personal gain but for advancing God's kingdom through miracles, healings, and deliverance. When believers walk in the Spirit, they can lay hands on the sick, cast out demons, and operate in the supernatural as a testimony of God's glory.

Biblical Example: Paul's Miraculous Ministry

Paul's ministry was characterized by extraordinary miracles. In Acts 19:11-12, "God did extraordinary miracles through Paul, so that even handkerchiefs and aprons that had touched him were taken to the sick, and their illnesses were cured, and the evil spirits left them." This manifestation of the Spirit's power affirmed Paul's ministry and led many to salvation. Living by the Spirit makes us vessels through which God demonstrates His power on earth.

VICTORY OVER SIN AND THE FLESH

Living by the Spirit enables believers to overcome sin and the desires of the flesh, cultivating a life of holiness and righteousness. Paul instructs, "Walk by the Spirit, and you will not gratify the desires of the flesh" (Galatians 5:16). The Spirit empowers believers to resist temptation, break free from sinful patterns, and build godly character. This victory is not achieved by human effort alone but through a continual surrender to the Spirit's guidance and strength. By relying on the Spirit, believers experience a transformation in their thoughts, actions, and desires, enabling them to walk in the freedom and purity that God intends.

Biblical Example: Joseph's Integrity

Joseph, son of Jacob, exemplified victory over sin and unwavering faithfulness to God. When tempted by Potiphar's wife, he refused to compromise his integrity, declaring, "How then could I do such a wicked thing and sin against God?" (Genesis 39:9). His ability to resist temptation stemmed from his deep devotion to God and the empowerment of the Spirit. Despite facing false accusations and imprisonment, Joseph remained steadfast, and in due time, God elevated him to a position of great authority in Egypt. His story serves as a powerful testament that those who live by the Spirit will not only walk in integrity but will also experience divine promotion, favor, and purpose fulfillment.

DIVINE WISDOM AND UNDERSTANDING

The Holy Spirit imparts wisdom and revelation, granting believers the ability to navigate life with divine insight and clarity. Isaiah 11:2 describes the Spirit as "the Spirit of wisdom and understanding, the Spirit of counsel and might, the Spirit of knowledge and the fear of the Lord." When individuals live by the Spirit, they gain supernatural discernment that enables them to perceive beyond natural limitations, make strategic decisions, and lead with godly wisdom. This divine guidance impacts personal choices and extends to leadership, conflict resolution, and problem-solving, equipping believers to fulfill their callings with excellence and effectiveness.

Biblical Example: Solomon's Divine Wisdom

Solomon's wisdom was unparalleled because he sought God's guidance. In 1 Kings 3:9, Solomon prayed, "Give your servant a discerning heart to govern your people and to distinguish between right and wrong." God granted his request, and Solomon became renowned for his wisdom, as evidenced by his judgments and writings in Proverbs and Ecclesiastes. His story demonstrates that we gain insight beyond human comprehension when we seek the Spirit's wisdom.

PEACE AND JOY IN THE MIDST OF TRIALS

A Spirit-led life is marked by supernatural peace and joy, even in adversity. Romans 14:17 states, "For the kingdom of God is not a matter of eating and drinking, but of righteousness, peace, and joy in the Holy Spirit." The Holy Spirit provides inner tranquility that surpasses understanding (Philippians 4:7), allowing believers to endure trials with unwavering faith. This peace is not dependent on circumstances but is a divine assurance that guards the heart and mind of the believer. It is the same peace that enabled Jesus to sleep through a storm (Mark 4:38-39) and sustained Paul through countless tribulations (2

Corinthians 11:23-28). Likewise, this joy is not mere happiness based on external conditions but a deep, abiding contentment found in God's presence (Psalm 16:11). When we live by the Spirit, we access a supernatural resilience that allows us to remain steadfast, hopeful, and victorious even in the face of life's greatest challenges.

Biblical Example: Paul and Silas in Prison

Paul and Silas' imprisonment in Philippi serves as a powerful illustration of how living by the Spirit grants believers supernatural strength, peace, and deliverance even in dire circumstances. After casting out a spirit of divination from a slave girl, they were falsely accused, beaten, and thrown into prison (Acts 16:16-24). Rather than succumbing to despair, they chose to pray and sing hymns to God, demonstrating their unwavering trust in the Holy Spirit's power (Acts 16:25).

Their praise became a catalyst for divine intervention. Suddenly, a great earthquake shook the prison, opening all the doors and unshackling every prisoner (Acts 16:26). This miraculous event not only led to their release but also to the salvation of the jailer and his household (Acts 16:27-34). Their Spirit-led resilience exemplifies how faith and joy in adversity can lead to supernatural breakthroughs and impact those around us. Paul and Silas' story reinforces the truth that living by the Spirit enables believers to triumph over suffering, maintain peace in trials, and serve as instruments of God's redemptive work. In Acts 16:25, Paul and Silas, despite being beaten and imprisoned, prayed and sang hymns to God. Their joy in suffering was a testament to the Holy Spirit's work in them, ultimately leading to a miraculous prison break and the salvation of the jailer's household. This account highlights that living by the Spirit produces a joy that is independent of circumstances.

SPIRITUAL GIFTS FOR MINISTRY

The Holy Spirit bestows spiritual gifts for the edification of the church (1 Corinthians 12:7-11). These gifts—such as prophecy, healing, and discernment—equip believers to serve effectively in their divine calling. A Spirit-led life is one of purpose, as believers are empowered to fulfill God's mission.

Biblical Example: Stephen's Boldness and Wisdom

Stephen, described as "a man full of faith and of the Holy Spirit" (Acts 6:5), was empowered to perform miracles and eloquently defend the faith. His Spirit-led wisdom confounded his opponents, proving the effectiveness of spiritual gifts in ministry. His story encourages believers to embrace their spiritual gifts and boldly proclaim the Gospel.

THE CALL TO LIVE BY THE SPIRIT

Living by the Spirit is not optional for believers—it is the essence of true Christianity. The Spirit provides guidance, transformation, power, victory over sin, divine wisdom, peace, joy, and spiritual gifts. The lives of Philip, Peter, Paul, Joseph, Solomon, and Stephen illustrate the profound impact of a Spirit-led life.

As we walk in the Spirit, we experience the fullness of God's presence and power, fulfilling our divine purpose. This journey of faith is not merely about avoiding sin but about actively embracing the richness of God's promises, walking in His divine favor, and bearing the fruit of righteousness. The Spirit shapes our character, aligns our desires with God's will, and empowers us to operate in His supernatural strength. Through the Spirit, we gain divine insight, experience miraculous breakthroughs, and cultivate a heart that remains steadfast in the face of trials. The invitation is open to all believers: "Since we live by the Spirit, let us keep in step with the Spirit" (Galatians 5:25). By doing so, we not only secure our spiritual inheritance but also become conduits of God's grace and power, transforming the world around us through His love and wisdom.

References

- Holy Bible, New International Version (NIV)
- MacArthur, J. (2003). *The Gospel According to Jesus: What Is Authentic Faith?* Zondervan.
- Piper, J. (2013). *Finally Alive: What Happens When We Are Born Again?* Crossway.
- Whitney, D. S. (2014). *Spiritual Disciplines for the Christian Life*. NavPress.
- Owen, J. (2006). *The Mortification of Sin*. Banner of Truth.

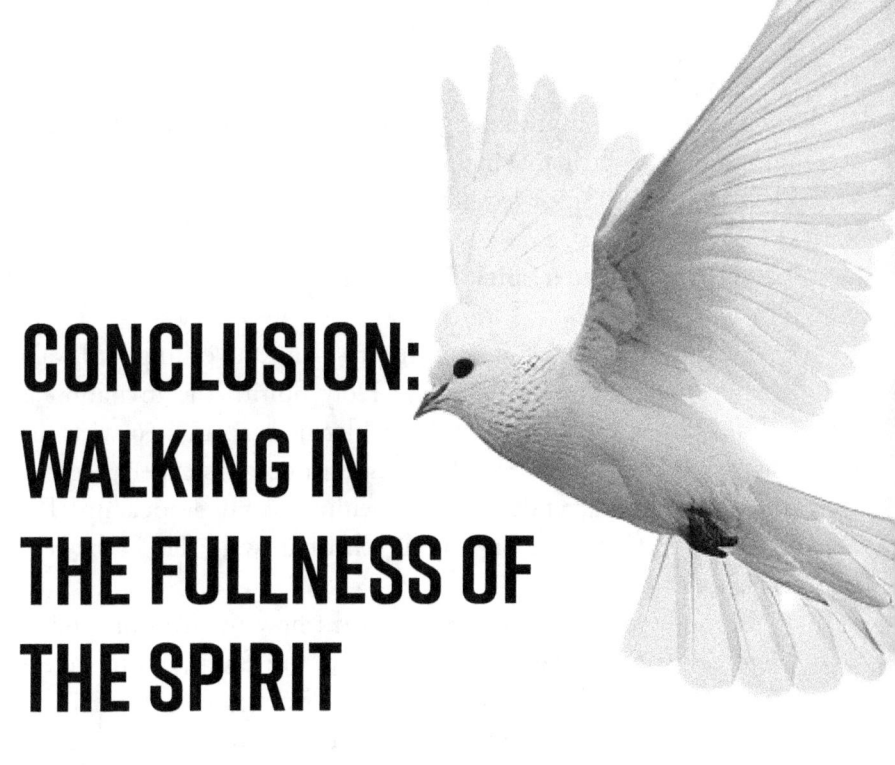

CONCLUSION: WALKING IN THE FULLNESS OF THE SPIRIT

Conclusion: Walking in the Fullness of the Spirit

As we come to the end of this journey through Living By The Spirit, it is important to reflect on the profound truth woven throughout these pages—our life in Christ is meant to be lived in the fullness of the Holy Spirit. From the moment of salvation to the daily walk of faith, the Spirit of God is the source of our power, transformation, and ultimate victory.

Living by the Spirit is not just an abstract theological concept; it is a practical and dynamic reality that influences every aspect of our lives. We have explored the essential doctrines of spiritual rebirth, the baptism of the Holy Spirit, and the importance of developing spiritual habits. We have examined the Spirit's power in overcoming sin, engaging in spiritual warfare, exercising spiritual gifts, and producing the fruit of righteousness. These are not merely doctrinal principles—they form the very foundation of a victorious, Spirit-led life.

The Invitation to a Spirit-Filled Life

Every believer has the opportunity—and the calling—to walk in intimate fellowship with the Holy Spirit. The invitation is clear: "Since we live by the Spirit, let us keep in step with the Spirit" (Galatians 5:25). This is not a one-time experience but a continuous surrender, a daily yielding to His leadership. The Spirit is not an accessory to our Christian walk; He is the very essence of it.

Throughout this book, we have seen how the lives of biblical figures were radically transformed by the Spirit. From Peter's boldness to Paul's miraculous ministry, from Joseph's integrity to Stephen's wisdom, each of these men lived with a deep awareness of the Spirit's guidance. Their lives were marked by divine encounters, supernatural strength, and an unwavering faith that changed the course of history.

Likewise, the same Spirit that empowered them is available to every believer today. God does not call us to a life of striving in our own strength but to one of resting in His Spirit, allowing Him to work in and through us.

A Call to Action: Pursue a Deeper Walk with the Spirit

This book is not just about gaining knowledge; it is about application. As you close these pages, I challenge you to evaluate your walk with the Holy Spirit:

1. Are you daily surrendering to the Spirit's leadership?
2. Are you growing in the fruit of the Spirit?

3. Are you walking in the power of the Spirit, using your spiritual gifts for God's glory?
4. Are you actively resisting sin and engaging in spiritual warfare?
5. Are you pursuing a life of holiness, intimacy, and divine purpose?

The answer to these questions will determine the depth of your spiritual walk. Living by the Spirit is not a passive experience; it is an active pursuit. The more you seek Him, the more you will experience His power, guidance, and presence in your life.

The Reward of Living by the Spirit

There is no greater life than one lived in the power of the Holy Spirit. It is a life of peace in the midst of chaos, joy in the face of trials, wisdom in difficult decisions, and power to overcome the works of the enemy. It is a life that reflects the glory of Christ and bears witness to His kingdom.

Jesus promised, "But you will receive power when the Holy Spirit comes on you; and you will be my witnesses in Jerusalem, and in all Judea and Samaria, and to the ends of the earth" (Acts 1:8). That promise is for you.

As you move forward, let this truth be the guiding force of your life: You were created to walk in the Spirit. You were called to live in the power of God. You were chosen to reflect the character of Christ.

Let nothing hinder you from stepping into the fullness of what God has prepared for you. The Spirit is calling. The Father is waiting. The kingdom is advancing. Will you walk in the Spirit?

May your life be a testimony of the transforming power of the Holy Spirit. May you be counted among those who live, walk, and move in the Spirit of the Living God.

"Now to Him who is able to do immeasurably more than all we ask or imagine, according to His power that is at work within us, to Him be glory in the church and in Christ Jesus throughout all generations, forever and ever! Amen." (Ephesians 3:20-21)

ABOUT THE AUTHOR

Antonio M. Palmer

Bishop Antonio M. Palmer is the Senior Pastor of Kingdom Celebration Center and the Presiding Bishop of Kingdom Alliance of Churches International, overseeing a global network of 74 churches. With a ministry rooted in the Gospel since 1993, he planted his first church in Annapolis, Maryland, in 1995 and has since become a beacon of leadership, service, and transformation.

A passionate advocate for missions, Bishop Palmer leads leadership conferences, plants churches, and provides humanitarian aid to thousands of children in need across the globe. His work includes substantial financial support for orphanages in India and East Africa, demonstrating a steadfast commitment to serving the underserved.

A respected community leader, Bishop Palmer is celebrated for fostering unity and collaboration among diverse groups. His efforts focus on addressing critical issues, promoting meaningful dialogue, and inspiring transformative change. He holds a Bachelor of Divinity and a Master's in Pastoral Counseling and has been recognized with numerous accolades, including two Governor Citations, two County Executive Citations, and the prestigious Martin Luther King Jr. Drum Major Award.

Bishop Palmer's leadership extends beyond the pulpit. He has served as President of the United Black Clergy of Anne Arundel County and as a community representative for the Severn

Intergenerational Center. He serves on the Community Action Agency Board and has been a member of the United Way of Central Maryland RUN Board. His extensive collaboration with the County Executive's Office and community partners has focused on social justice, violence interruption, and equity.

Key Highlights of Bishop Palmer's Work:

- Advisor to the County Recovery Workgroup.
- Partnered with the Caucus of African American Leaders to advocate for media equity.
- Organized the "1000 Men March," a peaceful protest against racism that united 26 civic organizations and elected officials.
- Led COVID-19 response efforts through partnerships with the Anne Arundel County Health Department, including organizing testing sites and running remote learning programs for underserved communities.
- Oversees a food distribution program that serves over 1,000 individuals weekly.

As an entrepreneur, Bishop Palmer owns **Kingdom Publishing LLC**, **Antonio Marlin Art**, and **Kingdom Kare, Inc.**, a thriving nonprofit organization. He is also the author of six impactful books and two workbooks with teacher manuals:

Books
- *Living By the Spirit*
- *Love Thyself: Empowering Men for Healthy Living*
- *God's Rest Revealed: A Life Flowing with Milk and Honey*
- *Building an Effective Prayer Life*

- *Mark the Perfect Man: How to Find a Model of Maturity*
- *Revival: God Will Come Where You Are*
- *Little Kairo Conquers the World (Children's Book)*

Workbooks
- *Introductory to Spiritual Warfare*
- *Living By the Spirit*

Bishop Palmer's ministry is enriched by the love and partnership of his wife of 31 years, Dr. Barbara Palmer. Together, they share a legacy of faith, wisdom, and joy with their son Randy, daughter-in-law Kimberly, and five cherished grandchildren.

Author's contact information:

Email:

apalmerkcc@gmail.com
bishopkccodenton@gmail.com
apalmer@kingdomkareinc.com

Websites:

Artwork: https://antoniomarlin.art
Publishing: www.mykingdompublishing.com
Church: www.kingdomcelebrationcenter.com
Kingdom Kare, Inc: www.kingdomkareinc.com

www.ingramcontent.com/pod-product-compliance
Lightning Source LLC
Chambersburg PA
CBHW061657120626
46550CB00003B/973